The Religion–Gender Nexus in Development

This book illuminates the intersection of religion and gender within the development sector, exposing challenges in both policy and practice and suggesting implementable solutions.

This book argues that a better understanding of the religion–gender nexus is needed by development sector practitioners, especially at a time when religious arguments are being used around the world to justify gender inequality and violence against women. The book draws on extensive qualitative research with senior gender personnel, religion advisors, and implementation partners from across the largest bilateral development agencies. The nexus is considered from the grassroots level up to donor country politics and across key themes, such as gender-based violence, reproductive rights, unpaid care and domestic work, and women's participation in leadership roles. The book concludes by offering implementable solutions for practitioners to address the religion–gender nexus in a more meaningful way.

Bridging the gap between academic theory and day-to-day development practice, this book is an important reference for development practitioners, and for researchers from across development studies, gender studies, and religious studies.

Nora Khalaf-Elledge is a gender and development practitioner and a Postdoctoral Fellow at the Faith & Civil Society Unit at Goldsmiths, University of London. She specialises in the intersection of religion and gender within international development policy and practice. Since 2008, she has worked with international development organisations including the Institute of Development Studies (IDS), the International Partnership on Religion and Sustainable Development (PaRD), the German Development Agency (GIZ), the Joint Learning Initiative on Faith and Local Communities (JLI), Development Alternatives Inc. (DAI), as well as the gender offices of multiple United Nations (UN) agencies. Nora holds a PhD in Gender, Religion and Development from the University of London, a Master's in Gender and Development from IDS, and a Bachelor's in Anthropology and Development from the University of Sussex.

Routledge Research in Religion and Development
Series Editors:
Matthew Clarke, *Deakin University, Australia*
Emma Tomalin, *University of Leeds, UK*
Nathan Loewen, *University of Alabama, USA*
Editorial board:
Carole Rakodi, *University of Birmingham, UK*
Gurharpal Singh, *School of Oriental and African Studies,*
University of London, UK
Jörg Haustein, *School of Oriental and African Studies,*
University of London, UK
Christopher Duncanson-Hales, *Saint Paul University, Canada*

The *Routledge Research in Religion and Development* series focuses on the diverse ways in which religious values, teachings and practices interact with international development.

While religious traditions and faith-based movements have long served as forces for social innovation, it has only been within the last ten years that researchers have begun to seriously explore the religious dimensions of international development. However, recognising and analysing the role of religion in the development domain is vital for a nuanced understanding of this field. This interdisciplinary series examines the intersection between these two areas, focusing on a range of contexts and religious traditions.

Adapting Gender and Development to Local Religious Contexts
A Decolonial Approach to Domestic Violence in Ethiopia
Romina Istratii

Human Development and the Catholic Social Tradition
Towards an Integral Ecology
Séverine Deneulin

The Religion–Gender Nexus in Development
Policy and Practice Considerations
Nora Khalaf-Elledge

For more information about this series, please visit: www.routledge.com/
Routledge-Research-in-Religion-and-Development/book-series/RRRD

The Religion–Gender Nexus in Development

Policy and Practice Considerations

Nora Khalaf-Elledge

R Routledge
Taylor & Francis Group

LONDON AND NEW YORK

First published 2022
by Routledge
2 Park Square, Milton Park, Abingdon, Oxon OX14 4RN

and by Routledge
605 Third Avenue, New York, NY 10158

Routledge is an imprint of the Taylor & Francis Group, an informa business

© 2022 Nora Khalaf-Elledge

The right of Nora Khalaf-Elledge to be identified as author of this work has been asserted by her in accordance with sections 77 and 78 of the Copyright, Designs and Patents Act 1988.

British Library Cataloguing-in-Publication Data
A catalogue record for this book is available from the British Library

Library of Congress Cataloging-in-Publication Data
Names: Khalaf-Elledge, Nora, editor.
Title: The religion–gender nexus in development : policy and practice considerations / edited by Nora Khalaf-Elledge.
Description: Abingdon, Oxon ; New York, NY : Routledge, 2021. | Series: Routledge research in religion and development | Includes bibliographical references and index.
Subjects: LCSH: Sex discrimination against women—Religious aspects. | Women—Violence against. | Women's rights.
Classification: LCC HQ1237 .R46 2021 (print) | LCC HQ1237 (ebook) | DDC 323.3/4—dc23
LC record available at https://lccn.loc.gov/2021016552
LC ebook record available at https://lccn.loc.gov/2021016553

ISBN: 978-0-367-63232-8 (hbk)
ISBN: 978-0-367-63234-2 (pbk)
ISBN: 978-1-003-11254-9 (ebk)

DOI: 10.4324/9781003112549

For Eleanor, light of my life.

Contents

Figures

Acknowledgements

This book would not have been possible without the kindness and support of my colleagues, friends, and family, and of course, all the development practitioners and activists who shared their time and insights so generously.

I express my sincere gratitude to my academic advisors and colleagues, especially Prof. Abby Day and Prof. Adam Dinham, for their invaluable support and mentorship throughout this research journey. I would also like to thank Prof. Christopher Baker, Dr Naomi Thompson, Dr David Hirsh, Prof. Emma Tomalin, and Dr Katherine Robinson for their insightful feedback on earlier versions of this work.

I would like to thank my friends and family – because no one achieves anything alone. I am grateful to my siblings, my grandmother, my grand-aunt, my parents in-law, and my dear friends. I feel deep gratitude to my loving and supporting parents: my mother, who taught me about courage, women's rights, and being myself. Her stories instilled in me a fascination about the study of religion and gender. And my father, for teaching me about international development, for daring me to be adventurous, and for always making me laugh. You have both been an immense source of inspiration and energy to me throughout the writing of this book.

Last but not least, I am grateful to my husband, best friend, and one-person-support-miracle. You have been with me from the very first words to the last words of this book. Thank you for your unwavering support and motivational speeches, our impromptu brainstorming sessions, dinnertime discussions, and long walks in the park. I am so lucky to have you. You are my rock.

Introduction

Over the past two decades, development organisations have joined arms with religious actors on issues like healthcare, humanitarian assistance, access to finance, peacebuilding, education, and gender equality. But gender is not just *one* of these issues. When it comes to religion and development, gender can easily be considered *the* issue. Religious beliefs and practices play a key role in shaping gender roles within societies. They have inspired both patriarchal and emancipatory changes. Sociologists have long acknowledged the global occurrence and relevance of this interplay. For example, Casanova (2009: 17) proclaims:

> The religious politics of gender has become one of the most important issues facing humanity worldwide and is likely to remain an issue of increasing relevance for the foreseeable future.

Casanova (2009: 15), among others, notes the 'obsessive focus on sexual moral issues' of political religion (also Loaeza, 2009). Whenever religion enters the public sphere or becomes powerful in politics, it tends to orbit around gender issues. Political religion focuses on gender because gender norms define the power structures of a community. Gender norms can preserve traditional divisions of labour and maintain the status quo. Patriarchal gender norms are packaged in the language of religion because it legitimises them, making them seem divinely ordained and unchangeable. Political religion's favourite issues include same-sex marriage, reproductive health, and sex education. Religious arguments continue to be used to condone domestic violence, marital rape, child marriage, and female genital mutilation. It is worth noting that patriarchal interpretations of religions discriminate not just against women but people of any gender if their behaviour or appearance is considered to be at odds with traditional norms. Political authorities, in high- and low-income countries alike, propagate the

DOI: 10.4324/9781003112549-1

idea that patriarchy and religion are inseparable. It gives them votes, it gives them power, and it plays into deeply held social norms.

This global (re)emergence of political religion has been interpreted as a direct patriarchal response to the perceived threat of gender equality, feminism, and the emancipation of women (Riesebrodt, 2000). Given the global occurrence of the religion–gender nexus, it is time that development practitioners acknowledge the need to engage critically and directly with this intersection. Development organisations face difficulties implementing projects in communities where they have systematically neglected, misunderstood, or perpetuated patriarchal dynamics of the religion–gender nexus. Development practice increasingly relies on faith partnerships[1] but has been slow to address the gender implications of those partnerships. Additionally, there is little acknowledgement of how donor countries' own religious politics have influenced gendered development efforts. If development continues to ignore this issue, it perpetuates the dangerous confusion of religion and patriarchy which not only obstructs gender equality but also sacralises it. Perhaps worst of all, it betrays all those who fight hard every day to reinterpret religious texts and reform unjust laws.

This book aims to assist practitioners as well as policymakers and researchers to navigate the complex intersection of religion and gender in development. The book introduces a change in theorising the religion–gender nexus by situating it within the gender domain of development and the wider power balances of the sector. To date, development has conceptualised the intersection of gender and religion primarily as a by-product of development's partnerships with religious actors rather than a topic of analysis in its own right. The book explores the religion–gender nexus as a phenomenon that transcends developed versus developing country binaries and highlights the complex roles religions play in shaping gendered norms and power dynamics in both donor and recipient countries. The book focuses on the themes of the UN Sustainable Development Goal (SDG) number five, specifically gender-based discrimination, gender-based violence, child marriage and female genital mutilation, and sexual and reproductive health rights and access.

The book situates the religion–gender discussion within the gender and development (GAD) debate. It argues that, that in order for development to appropriately address the religion–gender nexus, GAD has to be better implemented overall. The gender and development (GAD) approach was announced in 1995 at the Fourth World Conference on Women in Beijing. It was intended to replace its predecessor, the women in development (WID) approach, which was introduced in the 1970s and marked the first time the role of women in international development was recognised and discussed. Nevertheless, WID was materialistic and instrumentalist in nature. It focused exclusively on women and only on the economic dimension of their exclusion from development processes. WID instrumentalised women for other development goals rather than promoting equality as an end in itself. Consequently, the GAD approach set out to focus on the socially constructed basis of gender roles and the structural inequalities of gender relations. In practice, however, the GAD approach is merely a name change. Gender initiatives in development continue to focus on women in isolation and offer materialistic solutions to their subordinated roles. The research presented in this book finds that closing the gap between GAD theory and practice must take place prior to forming religious partnerships, which have been the modus operandi of addressing religion in development over the past two decades. A reliance on external partnerships caters to development's preference of efficiency, political expedience, and the outsourcing of religious literacy, but can have gender-regressive effects and perpetuates the notion of religion as an isolated category unique to developing countries. Meanwhile, rushed gender analyses or insufficient attention to gender reporting neglect the complex ways in which religions interact with gender norms. The book demonstrates that a comprehensive, context-specific, and theory-based gender analysis can highlight the religion–gender intersection in a given locality and facilitate the inclusion of religious actors. It can also uncover the patriarchal power dynamics behind religious arguments. Although GAD does currently not explicitly mention religion, it lays the foundation for an intersectional study of gender and the power structures surrounding gender norms and roles. However, current institutional power imbalances and practitioners' attitudes have kept intersectional subjects like religion and gender at the margin of the discipline. Feminist writers have thus called for the decolonisation of development. They argue that development must be seen as a global project rather than a Western service. This entails ending the idea of the 'Western expert' and conceptions of religions as either regressive or an instrument for development. A decolonial GAD approach would recognise that feminist movements do not only exist in the West and that gender discrimination and political religion is not unique to the Global South.

The book consists of two parts: Part I discusses *why* the religion–gender nexus matters in development and the extent to which it has been addressed in current development policy and practice. Part II explores *how* to integrate the religion–gender nexus into development approaches. It focuses on four areas: building religious literacy, implementing holistic and theory-based gender analyses, confronting practitioners' attitudes and biases,[2] and creating enabling environments for change agents. The book seeks to equip the reader with the tools necessary to make sense of the complex ways in which gender and religion interact and how sociopolitical circumstances can exacerbate this dynamic. For example, it demonstrates that analysing gender norms across the three lenses of power, performance, and policing is particularly relevant for practitioners to produce a holistic yet nuanced analysis that avoids religious generalisation and simplifications. The book combines post-structural feminist theory with postcolonial and decolonial development critiques to highlight current barriers within the development sector to addressing the religion–gender nexus and offers implementable suggestions for practitioners. The end goal is to help practitioners reduce bias in their own gender work, to identify institutional power dynamics that have marginalised the GAD agenda, and to work in partnership with religious actors without using them as substitutes for internal religious literacy or further marginalising feminist local voices.

The argument developed in this book is based on research conducted as part of a doctoral study between 2015 and 2019. The study followed a qualitative approach and used a concurrent triangulation method involving three different levels of development practitioners. Data were collected through semi-structured interviews which were recorded and transcribed verbatim, as well as an in-depth document analysis of government aid agencies' policy and programme reporting. A concurrent triangulation method was used to confirm and cross-check the validity of findings more widely and provide a fuller picture. By including both high-level and ground-level organisations, the research also intends to better understand and contrast needs, lived realities, challenges, and opportunities of actors at different levels[3]:

1   Eight government aid agency participants were primarily selected based on their total government spending on development aid (World Economic Forum, 2016), the extent of their gender programming[4] (OECD, 2017), whether or not they already mention religion in their written reporting, and finally, on their availability and willingness to take part. Government aid agency participants were all senior or directing gender advisors of respective agencies. Representatives of departments managing religious partnerships – where they existed – also participated.

2   Eight recipient organisations were selected based on active and past contracts with one or more of the government aid agencies selected for this study.[5] All recipient organisations have a long history of implementing programmes for participating government aid agencies and are currently actively implementing programmes funded by at least one of the governments studied in this research.

3   Eight local women's rights activists were selected based on their geographic location in at least one of the country contexts in which government aid agencies selected for this study were active and their track record of working towards equality in their locality. Most local activists had previously collaborated with government-funded development programmes as short-term consultants and thus could provide meaningful perspectives.

The countries covered through the interviews were aligned with the respective 'priority countries' of the government aid agencies selected for this research. Such 'priority countries' typically receive the most funding and attention from government aid agencies. The religious contexts of participant and project locations spanned regional variations of Hinduism, Christianity, and Islam in both high- and low-income countries. The conceptual focus was on patriarchal systems because most societies today are in practice patriarchal – even if not explicitly defined to be by their own constitutions and laws. Interview responses were recorded, transcribed verbatim, and imported into a qualitative data analysis programme (NVivo), where – together with the document analysis – they were coded using thematic analysis. The document analysis consisted of a rigorous and systematic analysis of 92 policy documents of both donor and recipient organisations and functioned as another form of cross-validation of interview data. It is important to note that many organisations use the terms 'culture', 'religion', and occasionally even 'social norms' interchangeably in their reporting.[6]

For the purpose of this book, the term 'gender' refers to the norms, roles, behaviours, and attributes through which a society defines masculinity and femininity. These expectations are not static but continually constructed and reinforced through societal power dynamics. The usage of the term 'feminism' does not imply allegiance to a specific political strand or ideology but to the belief that women and men should be equal in society and before the law. The term religion is used in a Durkheimian fashion, referring to a set of beliefs that have a social function, yet with a Weberian interest in how religion can construct and legitimate power, as well as generate social change. My analysis is particularly interested in current empirical – largely women-led – research on religion as a *lived* concept and its gendered dimension (e.g., McGuire, 2008; Sharafeldin, 2013; Bishop, 2016; Day, 2017). Finally, the ultimate purpose of this research is to explore how religion is understood in gender approaches and by practitioners themselves, and what impact such conceptions have on development activities.

This book uses 'religion' rather than 'faith' throughout, except in cases where it cites other work, refers to existing programmes, or uses the technical term faith-based organisations (FBOs). The book uses the term 'religious partnerships' to refer to partnerships with FBOs and religious actors. The definitions of the terms 'faith' and 'religion' in development literature currently lack clarity and consistency. At times they are used interchangeably, while at other times they are listed together as if they refer to two separate elements of the same entity, with neither one defined properly. This book uses 'religion' because of the misleading connotations of 'faith' and because it has little relevance outside of Western Christian tradition (Hefferan, 2015: 41). Faith, as used in bilateral development discourses, insinuates something personal and individualistic centred around practices and beliefs. Nevertheless, development has largely engaged with organised religion based on efficiency and service provision rather than an interest in the personal faith dimension of its beneficiaries. This book considers religion as a social force rather than as a personal experience. The book seeks to draw attention to the complex political and power dimensions of religion in the public sphere of both donor and recipient countries.

Notes

1 This is the most commonly used term to refer to partnerships with religious actors or faith-based organisations (FBOs). The book elaborates on the problems of this terminology, including the misleading connotations of 'faith' in development discourses in Chapter 4.
2 For the purpose of this book the term 'bias' refers to the preconceived notions of development practitioners towards intersectional concepts such as religion and gender and their coloured lenses through which they approach these subjects.
3 Qualitative research tends to work with smaller amounts of data. My research sample includes five of the largest government aid agencies and their implementing partner organisations. As such, it can be considered sufficiently representative of the current policy environment of international development. Due to confidentiality agreements, names of organisations cannot be made public as part of the research results. Names of interviewees have been changed.
4 The term 'gender programming' in this book refers to all development aspects, analyses, and activities concerned with gender throughout the development project cycle. The development project cycle typically consists of programme design, implementation, and evaluation.
5 The term 'Recipient organisations' refers to organisations that implement projects in developing countries through donor funding.
6 The subject of terminology was included in the interview questions. This is important to ensure data could be interpreted accurately.

Bibliography

Bishop, S. (2016). Troubling Essentialism: Studying Religion and Feminism. *The Religious Studies Project*. Available from: www.religiousstudiesproject. com/2016/10/13/troubling-essentialism-studying-religion-and-feminism/ [accessed 14 October 2020].
Casanova, J. (2009). Religion, Politics and Gender Equality: Public Religions Revisited. In S. Razavi (ed.), *A Debate on the Public Role of Religion and Its Social and Gender Implications*. Geneva: UN Research Institute for Social Development, Gender and Development Programme Paper No. 5.
Day, A. (2017). *The Religious Lives of Older Laywomen*. Oxford: Oxford University Press.
Hefferan, T. (2015). *Researching Religions and Development*. In E. Tomalin (ed.), *The Routledge Handbook on Religions and Global Development*. London and New York: Routledge.

Loaeza, S. (2009). Cultural Change in Mexico at the Turn of the Century: The Secularization of Women's Identity and the Erosion of the Authority of the Catholic Church. In F. Hagopian (ed.), *Religious Pluralism, Democracy, and the Catholic Church in Latin America*. Notre Dame, IN: University of Notre Dame Press.

McGuire, M. (2008). *Lived Religion: Faith and Practice in Everyday Life*. New York: Oxford University Press.

Organisation for Economic Cooperation and Development (OECD). (2017). *Aid in Support of Gender Equality and Women's Empowerment*. Available from: www. oecd.org/dac/stats/aidinsupportofgenderequalityandwomensempowerment.htm [accessed 3 June 2019].

Riesebrodt, M. (2000). Fundamentalism and the Resurgence of Religion. *Numen*, 47(3): 266–287.

Sharafeldin, M. (2013). Egyptian Women's Rights NGOs: Personal Status Law Reform Between Islamic and International Human Rights Law. In Z. Mir-Hosseini, K. Vogt, L. Larsen, and C. Moe (eds.), *Gender and Equality in Muslim Family Law*. London: I. B. Tauris.

World Economic Forum. (2016). *Foreign Aid: These Countries Are the Most Generous*. Available from: www.weforum.org/agenda/2016/08/foreign-aid-these-countries-are-the-most-generous/ [accessed 3 June 2019].

Part I

Why the religion–gender nexus matters in development

1 Religion and gender at the crossroads

Key concepts and theories

Religion and gender are deeply connected, and this chapter explores key concepts within their intersection. The discussion offers answers to the following questions: how are gender roles and relationships constructed in the context of religion, what drives the different treatment of men and women within religious traditions, and why are power and politics at the very centre of the religion–gender nexus? This chapter specifically focuses on the concepts of patriarchy, hegemonic masculinity, gender essentialism, and social constructionism. This chapter also covers the gender implications of rising religious fundamentalism and explores recent examples of religious feminism.

First and foremost, it is important to note how narrow existing literature on the religion–gender nexus is overall. Social sciences, including gender studies and religious studies, are yet to produce a dedicated research agenda on this intricate and dynamic interplay. The one area that has received ample interest, especially in Western discourses, is the gender differences in religiosity. Since the 1980s, social scientists in the West have been fascinated with the idea that women are more religious than men and have sought to explain this phenomenon (see Walter and Davie, 1998; Trzebiatowska and Bruce, 2012). However, the debate about who is more religious is at best inconclusive and at worst counterproductive:

> The tendency for predominantly male sociologists to pursue the idea that women are universally and ahistorically more religious than men [may in itself be an effort] to cement the idea that women are natural producers of subordinate femininity.
>
> (Day, 2017: 210)

In the absence of unbiased and empirically based research outside of Western Christian realms, a definitive global explanation of gender differences in

DOI: 10.4324/9781003112549-2

religiosity remains elusive. Rather than debating the gender gap of religiosity, this book is interested in how religion and its institutions and practices have shaped, mirrored, or masked gender roles and inequalities.

What drives gender inequality in religious traditions?

Gender inequality in religious traditions is produced by the same structures that maintain it anywhere. The fallacy that religion is more prone to gender inequality than other social systems continues to be widespread in development practice. To avoid reproducing this myth, I will not focus on specific religious traditions but instead review concepts central to the intersection of religion and gender. A conceptual focus recognises the context dependency and historical situatedness of religions, rather than making universal and timeless claims about individual religious traditions.

Patriarchy

The boundaries between patriarchy and religion are blurred. In patriarchal systems, religion is often invoked to legitimise existing power structures and maintain gender norms (Sultana, 2011: 14). In other words, religion can both condone and conceal patriarchy. Patriarchy then comes to be seen as a characteristic of religion, when it should be an object of analysis in its own right (Wilson, 2017). A focus on patriarchal power structures can shed light on the interaction of religion and gender (Woodhead, 2007: 557). Patriarchies are the most common gendered systems of power. Therefore, they are a key focus in feminist theory. Patriarchy is commonly defined as 'a system of social structures, and practices in which men dominate, oppress and exploit women' (Walby, 1990: 214). A more detailed definition is given by French (1985: 239):

> [Patriarchy consists in the] manifestation and institutionalization of male dominance over women and children in the family and the extension of male dominance over women in society in general. It implies that men hold power in all the important institutions of society and women are deprived of access to such power.

In other words, patriarchies are systems in which men are more likely to hold positions of social, economic, and political power than women. Already in 1948, Marx and Engels observed that the domination of women enables men to control production and property. Much of feminist theory on patriarchy is influenced by Marx's conceptualisation of social inequality. Feminist theory transferred Marxist ideas of class relations to male–female relations marking patriarchy as a key component of gender oppression (Wilson, 2000: 1493).

French's conceptualisation of patriarchy (1985: 239) centres around the key issue of structural inequality but does not imply that 'women are either totally powerless or totally deprived of rights, influences, and resources'. Women still have agency even in a system that is designed to deprioritise their interests. Moreover, women may also enact and benefit from patriarchal norms or support ideologies that are gender oppressive. Some patriarchal practices, such as female genital mutilation (FGM), are typically performed by women on women (Sultana, 2012; Monagan, 2010; Tomalin, 2007, also see Chapter 5). This understanding is important for development practitioners because there is still a widespread belief that increasing women's participation alone or partnering with women will automatically generate more 'women-friendly' results. Likewise, there is currently little understanding of what differentiates a women's organisation from a feminist one.

Hegemonic masculinity

Connell introduced the concept of 'hegemonic masculinities' to explain how men maintain dominance in societies (Connell, 1983[1]). Based on a Gramscian understanding of hegemony, the adjective *hegemonic* refers to keeping one social group in a superior position to another. Hegemonic masculinity refers to the collective learnt patterns of behaviour that perpetuate men's dominance over women. Connell and Messerschmidt (2005: 832) argue that while men feel compelled to live up to the ideal of hegemonic masculinity, they 'ideologically legitimated the global subordination of women'. It equally subordinates men who do not conform with prevalent masculinity ideals. The concept of hegemonic masculinity has received significant attention over the past three decades and has served as a framework for much of the emerging research effort on men and masculinity, arguably replacing conventional 'sex-role theory' and categorical models of patriarchy. Because the concept has been applied to diverse practical issues and cultural contexts, it has also attracted considerable criticism. Petersen (1998), among others, argued that the very core of the concept is flawed because it establishes a false sense of unity of the character of men contrary to a fluid and diverse reality. Similarly, others have posited that it is built upon a heteronormative conception of gender that oversimplifies male–female differences and excludes women from the analysis (Paechter, 2006).

The concept of hegemonic masculinity in the context of religion remains unexplored. Nevertheless, sociologists have observed patriarchal structures within many religions (Seguino, 2011; Klingorova and Havlicek, 2015).

Subsequently, these dynamics could also be explored through Connell's concept of hegemonic masculinity, particularly since the features of male dominance identified by sociologists across religious traditions resemble the hegemonic traits highlighted in Connell's theory. For example, monotheistic religions typically worship a God who is represented with male features (Klingorova and Havlicek, 2015). This does not mean that polytheistic religions and religions with goddesses are less patriarchal. Polytheism can be both empowering and oppressive for women depending on whether or not the patriarchal practices 'fool girls into believing that they are not worthy of the same reverence bestowed on a goddess' (Sarkar, 2014). The sacralising of male headship and female subordination in some religious interpretations may legitimise this hegemonic masculinity. Hegemonic masculinity, applied to the study of gender and religion, could help explain why certain gender ideals are promoted over others and how this maintains the social hierarchy. Connell's theory holds that these hierarchies are socially constructed and subject to change. The concept of hegemonic masculinity should therefore be of particular interest to feminist research in development as it allows for a 'struggle for hegemony'. This struggle could result in the elimination of gender hierarchies or the replacement of older forms of masculinity by newer, perhaps less oppressive, ones (Connell and Messerschmidt, 2005: 833).

Gender essentialism versus social constructionism

Gender essentialism refers to the idea that men and women are inherently different and that this difference is based on unique and natural attributes that qualify them as separate genders (Crompton and Lyonette, 2005: 601). Gender essentialism further stipulates that 'those characteristics defined as women's essence are shared in common by all women at all times' and that it is 'not possible for a subject to act in a manner contrary to her essence' (Crompton and Lyonette, 2005: 601). In other words, essentialist theories present a binary understanding of gender that pits all women against all men, and vice versa. The idea of gender essentialism can appear across different scientific disciplines. For example, gender essentialism may be sustained in biological arguments, suggesting that *maleness* and *femaleness* are driven by different levels of sex hormones (Baron-Cohen, 2004). The debate on gender differences in religiosity mentioned at the beginning of this chapter is to a large extent based on gender essentialist assumptions, painting women as inherently more vulnerable, nurturing, and risk-averse than their male counterparts. Any fundamentalist ideology, religious or otherwise, that is interested in maintaining traditional structures typically follows an essentialist worldview. Gender essentialism normalises gender differences and makes inequality seem 'natural' (Bourdieu, 1977: 164). As a result, feminist theory has identified gender essentialism as a major obstacle to social change and gender equality.

In contrast to gender essentialism, feminist theory suggests that most of the presumed differences between men and women are socially constructed and upheld in gender hierarchies and patterns of inequality (Crompton and Lyonette, 2005: 601). Social constructionist theory has provided the basis for feminist critiques of gender essentialism. Influenced by sociologists such as Berger and Luckmann (1966: 1) and Bourdieu (1977), social constructionism claims that reality and knowledge are created and learnt rather than innate (Berger and Luckmann, 1966: 1). Arbitrary invented social norms are naturalised through their continuous reproduction (Bourdieu, 1977: 164). Post-structural feminist philosopher Butler (1990) has applied this theory to the study of gender. Through her theory of 'gender performativity', she describes how individuals participate in the ongoing social construction of their gendered identity. Butler conceptualises gender as performative, which means that people enact their gender roles until they believe they were born with them. Butler's idea of gender performativity originates in de Beauvoir's claim that 'one is not born, but rather, becomes a woman' (de Beauvoir, 1952; Butler, 1988: 519). Social constructionist theory is vital to feminism because it draws attention to how gender norms are created to maintain social structures. Additionally, it offers pathways to change by asserting that gender relations are ever evolving and gender inequality is not set in stone.

Butler's work on gender has been applied across a variety of other fields. For example, gender performativity is used to explain the learning of gender roles in educational systems (see Arnot, 2002; Paechter, 2006; Campbell, 2010). Paechter (2006) explains that curricula are a primary source for teaching boys and girls how to enact masculinity and femininity and become 'gendered bodies' (Paechter, 2006). Similarly, Arnot posits that 'gender encoding' in education shapes social relations between girls and boys from early age onwards (Arnot, 2002). Boys and girls learn to distinguish clearly defined gender roles, the relationship between them, and the necessary character attributes to successfully achieve those (Campbell, 2010).

The concept of gender performativity remains under-analysed in the realm of religion. Some scholars, without referring to gender performativity, have engaged with the construction of gender roles in the context of religion. For example, Klingorova and Havlicek (2015) argue that – especially in patriarchal religious interpretations – gender roles frequently reflect essentialist thinking. Ideas of masculinity and femininity are constructed in opposition to each other: men should be dominant and women should be submissive; men are leaders, providers, household heads and women are followers, supporters, carers (Klingorova and Havlicek, 2015). The re-enactment of these ideas provides a critical foundation for male hegemony over women (see Cornwall, 1997; Connell, 1987). Development researchers Marcus and Harper (2015) also found that religious institutions and their leaders play a significant and complex role in defining essentialist gender norms as well as in shaping the roles and responsibilities of men and women in society. Their work suggests that religious values tend to emphasise gendered 'virtues' such as virginity for women, which in turn encourages early marriage and, as such, shapes girls' roles in society as future wives and mothers. Marcus and Harper's analysis is useful as it highlights the role of religion in the social construction of gender norms; however, it largely uses religion as a bland and stagnant category. A meaningful discussion of religion and gender must recognise religions' intricacies and context-specific expressions within exiting socio-historical power structures. In their fight against gender essentialism, development practitioners must be careful not to essentialise religion instead. Essentialising religion ignores the diverse lived expressions of religions. It legitimises context-specific interpretations of religion as timeless and universal and leaves little to no room for change.

Religious fundamentalisms

Gender essentialist worldviews are common in fundamentalist ideologies. The term 'fundamentalism' originated as part of a Protestant revival movement in the United States in the early 20th century that sought to return to the fundamentals of the Christian faith and a literal interpretation of the rules of the Bible (Woodberry and Smith, 1998). Since then, the term has been widely used in similar movements across different religious traditions, such as Judaism, Islam, and Hinduism (Armstrong, 2000; Almond et al., 2003; Imam et al., 2017[2]). A widely used definition of religious fundamentalism in academia was coined by Altemeyer and Hunsberger in 1992:

> The belief that there is one set of religious teachings that clearly contains the fundamental, basic, intrinsic, essential, inerrant truth about humanity and deity; that this essential truth is fundamentally opposed by the forces of evil which must be vigorously fought; that this truth must be followed today according to the fundamental, unchangeable practices of the past; and that those who believe and follow these fundamental teachings have a special relationship with the deity.
>
> (Altemeyer and Hunsberger, 1992: 118)

While fundamentalism started as a self-proclaimed identity, the politicisation of the term over the past few decades has added negative associations.[3] Many who are described as fundamentalists today would not necessarily identify themselves as such (Tomalin, 2007: 28). Fundamentalist expressions and interpretations of religions have been considered as a reactionary ideology to political or socio-economic changes within a given context. As Bruce (2008: 120) noted:

> [F]undamentalism is the rational response of traditionally religious people to social, political and economic changes that downgrade and constrain the role of religion in the public world.

Fundamentalism centres around the belief that gender identities and gender roles are biologically pre-determined. In other words, fundamentalism subscribes to gender essentialism.[4] In the case of religious fundamentalism, this determinism is backed up by textual tradition in which texts are to be taken literally, rather than interpreted according to societies' changing needs and circumstances (Tomalin, 2007: 18). Religious fundamentalism claims that gender differences are not only natural but also divinely ordained. This legitimises and sacralises gender inequality and leaves little to no room for change. Consequently, feminist scholars and activists have been wary of the increase of fundamentalist interpretations of religion.

Nevertheless, until the mid-1990s, little attention was paid to the gender effects of religious fundamentalisms. Some women's rights organisations, such as the Association for Women's Rights in Development' (AWID) and 'Women Against Fundamentalism' (WAF) have sought to correct this and shed light on how fundamentalist ideologies have spurred gender-based violence. Soon after its launch in 1989, WAF wrote:

> at the heart of all fundamentalist agendas is the control of women's minds and bodies. All religious fundamentalists support the patriarchal family as a central agent of such control. They view women as embodying the morals and traditional values of the family and the whole community.
>
> (Katz, for WAF, 1995: 42)

Shortly after, a research agenda emerged concerned with religious fundamentalism and its impact on gender equality and women's rights. For example, Riesebrodt (2000), among others, interpreted religious fundamentalism as a patriarchal reaction against the global threat of gender equality, secularism, and feminism. Fundamentalist groups tend to draw on the notion of an 'outside enemy' that threatens to spoil inside values and promote the 'the loosening of women' (Hawley and Proudfoot's, 1994: 27). Meanwhile, they view culture, family, and women as the only areas that remain within their control (Momsen, 2001: 51). Women's bodies subsequently become the main vehicles for maintaining traditional essentialist values (Katz, 1995: 42; Imam et al., 2017). For example, the Nigerian militant organisation Boko Haram bases itself on an ideology that accuses Western education of corrupting the modesty of young women and girls (Agbiboa and Maiangwa, 2013). Boko Haram's line of argument offers a critical foundation for maintaining male dominance over women and highlights the link between gender and fundamentalism. As the goal of gender equality becomes more widely accepted in society, fundamentalist interpretations can be expected to become more prevalent.

Some of this research has directly or indirectly implied that fundamentalism is more common in non-Western societies. For example, Hawley and Proudfoot argue that female emancipation is seen by many fundamentalists as 'a prominent feature of modern western secularism'. This situates *fundamentalists* outside of the West. Development literature has also focused on fundamentalism primarily in the Global South. But such gender ideologies have gained similar popularity in Western countries. There is a considerate body of literature concerned with the (re)emergence of religion in public politics in Europe and North America (Martin, 1990; Berger, 1999; Woodhead and Catto, 2012). Woodhead (2007: 564), for example, describes Western religious communities that attempt to defend 'traditional' roles for men and women embodied by male headship and female domesticity.

Religious feminism

Over the past decades, religious feminists and scholars of religion have provided a more nuanced understanding of the construction of gender norms in religious contexts. A body of literature emerged that powerfully rejects the idea that feminism and religion are mutually exclusive and that religion automatically oppresses women. For example, Christian feminists have argued that the Bible's gender unequal provisions do not stem from the text itself but are a result of the Christian male scholars who have interpreted the scripture throughout history. Some Christian feminists have abandoned direct scriptural use altogether in their fight for equality, while others highlight those Bible verses that challenge patriarchal ideals and men's privileged position in society (Mohrmann, 2015). The most recent and fastest-growing religious feminist discourse has arguably been Islamic feminism. In the following, I examine this example in detail to illustrate the dynamic and diverse roles religion may take in the struggle for gender equality.

Starting in the early 1990s, many feminists in the Middle East highlighted the inconsistency between Islamic values and the patriarchal systems in their countries. For the past two decades, they observed how a rising tide of fundamental Islamism across religious and political institutions led to the creation and preservation of laws that treat women as second-class citizens (Mir-Hosseini, 2013). Driven by the frustration over the systematic gendered discrimination in the name of religion, Islamic feminism[5] emerged as a new reform approach attempting to challenge the monopoly of religious legal knowledge production from within its system (Badran, 2011; Mir-Hosseini, 2013; Tadros, 2011). Islamic feminists have criticised governments' patriarchal interpretation of Islam and their disregard of Islamic provisions for women's rights within it (Mir-Hosseini, 2013). Scholars, such as Mernissi (1991), Ahmed (1992), Wadud (1994), Mir-Hosseini (2013), and Badran (2011), have reinterpreted Islamic sources and challenged many widely circulated but false *Hadiths* (sayings of the Prophet) (Mernissi, 1991). They seek reforms of religious laws based on the Islamic principles of justice, equality, and human dignity. Born from within the Islamic legal tradition, this newly created space for debate offers an internal critique of Islamic law in a way that has been unprecedented in Islamic history.

Islamic feminism has played a substantial role in bringing about recent reforms of religious family laws across the Middle East. For example, in 2004 Moroccan women's rights activists successfully appropriated Islamic arguments calling for a re-interpretation of Islamic sources and achieved a transformation of the ancient Muslim family law. Morocco is now the only country that has an Islamically backed egalitarian family law (Hursh, 2012). Morocco's case illustrates that religious laws are not immutable and that an egalitarian model of the family is possible within an Islamic framework (Badran, 2011). Compared to Morocco, Egyptian reform activists have received far less academic and international attention in their attempts to change discriminatory laws claimed on religious grounds. In Egypt, the biggest achievement of legal reform through religious activism has been the *Khul* divorce law. Since 2000, the *Khul* law gives women the right to initiate divorce, which previously required their husband's permission (Anwar et al., 2009: 32).[6]

Conclusion

The discussion in this chapter demonstrates that gender norms are continuously constructed, while religious interpretations can enforce, alter, or mirror current power dynamics. In some cases, religion has been employed as a political tool to sacralise and thereby conserve gendered power relations. At the same time, feminist movements within and outside of religious traditions have challenged gender discrimination claimed on religious grounds. The deep entanglement of religion and gender is a global phenomenon that shapes everyday life for billions of people. Its powerful and widespread influences are unlikely to disappear anytime soon. As such, this intersection merits development's immediate attention.

Notes

1 Connell's discussion was based on an Australian research study concerned with social inequality that provided empirical evidence of multiple gendered hierarchies linked to active processes of gender construction.
2 Imam et al. (2017) offer a useful overview of fundamentalist ideologies and their intersection with gender across different religions.
3 Some sociologists also avoid the term fundamentalism, noting it may imply a negative value judgement (see Davie, 2015: 183).
4 It is important to note that gender essentialist views also exist outside of fundamentalism and that women's bodies can also be a site of control in mainstream religion. Religious institutions reproduce social orders and play a big role in the lives of their members, including family planning decisions (Woodhead, 2007: 564, 2008).
5 Producers of this discourse do not always call themselves Islamic feminists. Many rejected the term 'feminism' because of its foreign stigma (Badran, 2011). Others prefer to be called Muslim feminists rather than Islamic feminists, stressing that while they believe Islam offers a credible framework for gender equality, they do not wish to create a state system entirely governed by Islamic law. Irrespective of their branding preferences, all writers are bound by their commitment to demonstrate that a discourse on gender equality is Islamically valid and advocate for the incorporation of gender as a category of thought into the production of religious knowledge (Mir-Hosseini, 2013).
6 The *Khul* law is based on an Islamic prophetic tradition that holds that a woman can divorce her husband unilaterally if she forgoes her financial rights. While a divorce through *Khul* deprives women of their financial rights, it gives them a way out of abusive marriages, which was not possible before. The prophetic injunction of *Khul* had been deliberately ignored by religious lawmakers and recently brought back to light by reform activists (Sholkamy, 2011).

Bibliography

Agbiboa, D. E., and Maiangwa, B. (2013). Boko Haram, Religious Violence, and the Crisis of National Identity in Nigeria Towards a Non-killing Approach. *Journal of Developing Societies*, 29(4): 379–403.
Ahmed, L. (1992). *Women and Gender in Islam*. Newhaven, London: Yale University Press.
Almond, G. A., Appleby, R. S., and Sivan, E. (2003). *Strong Religion: The Rise of Fundamentalisms Around the World*. Chicago, IL: Chicago University Press.
Altemeyer, B., and Hunsberger, B. (1992). Authoritarianism, Religious Fundamentalism, Quest, and Prejudice. *The International Journal for the Psychology of Religion*, 2(2): 113–133.

Anwar, Z., Rumminger, J., Mir-Hosseini, Z., and Balchin, C. (eds.). (2009). *Wanted. Equality and Justice in the Muslim Family.* Malaysia: Musawa.

Armstrong, K. (2000). *The Battle for God. Fundamentalism in Judaism, Christianity and Islam.* New York: Alfred Knopf.

Arnot, M. (2002). *Reproducing Gender: Critical Essays on Educational Theory and Feminist Politics.* Falmer: Routledge.

Badran, M. (2011). From Islamic Feminism to a Muslim Holistic Feminism. *IDS Bulletin,* 42(1): 78–87. Oxford: Blackwell Publishing.

Baron-Cohen, S. (2004). *The Essential Difference.* Harmondsworth, Middlesex: Penguin.

Berger, P. L. (ed.). (1999). *The Desecularization of the World.* Grand Rapids: William B. Eerdman's.

Berger, P. L., and Luckmann, T. (1966). *The Social Construction of Reality. A Treatise in the Sociology of Knowledge.* New York: Penguin Books.

Bourdieu, P. (1977). *Outline of a Theory of Practice.* Cambridge: Cambridge University Press.

Bruce, S. (2008). Fundamentalism. 2nd Ed. Cambridge: Polity Press.

Butler, J. (1988). Performative Acts and Gender Constitution: An Essay in Phenomenology and Feminist Theory. *Theatre Journal,* 4.

Butler, J. (1990). *Gender Trouble: Feminism and the Subversion of Identity.* London: Routledge.

Campbell, E. (2010). *Women in the History's Textbooks.* Available from: www.education.com/reference/article/womens-history-textbooks/?page=4 [accessed 26 September 2018].

Connell, R. W. (1983). *Which Way Is Up? Essays on Sex, Class and Culture.* Sydney, Australia: Allen and Unwin.

Connell, R. W. (1987). *Gender and Power.* Sydney, Australia: Allen and Unwin.

Connell, R. W., and Messerschmidt, J. W. (2005). Hegemonic Masculinity: Rethinking the Concept. *Gender & Society,* 19: 829–859.

Cornwall, A. (1997). Men, Masculinities and 'Gender in Development. *Gender and Development,* 5(2): 8–13. Taylor & Francis, Ltd. on behalf of Oxfam GB.

Crompton, R., and Lyonette, C. (2005). The New Gender Essentialism – Domestic and Family Choices' and Their Relation to Attitudes. *British Journal of Sociology,* 56(4): 601–624.

Davie, G. (2015). *Religion in Britain: A Persistent Paradox.* Oxford: Wiley-Blackwell.

Day, A. (2017). *The Religious Lives of Older Laywomen.* Oxford: Oxford University Press.

de Beauvoir, S. (1952). *The Second Sex* (H. M. Parshley, Trans.). New York: Random House.

French, M. (1985). *Beyond Power. On Women, Men, and Morals.* New York: Summit.

Hawley, J. S., and Proudfoot, W. (1994). *Fundamentalism and Gender.* Oxford: Oxford University Press.

Hursh, J. (2012). *Advancing Women's Rights Through Islamic Law: The Example of Morocco. Gender, Law Justice.* Berkeley: University of California Press.

Imam, A., Gokal, S., and Marler, I. (2017). The Devil is in the Details: A Feminist Perspective on Development, Women's Rights, and Fundamentalisms. *Gender and Development,* 25(1): 15–36.

Katz, S. (1995). The Rise of Religious Fundamentalism in Britain: The Experience of Women Against Fundamentalism. *Gender and Development*, 3(1): 42–44.

Klingorova, K., and Havlicek, T. (2015). Religion and Gender Inequality: The Status of Women in the Societies of World Religions. *Moravian Geographical Reports*, 23.

Marcus, R., and Harper, C. (2015). How Do Gender Norms Change? *Overseas Development Institute*. Available from: www.odi.org/sites/odi.org.uk/files/odi-assets/publications . . . files/9817.pdf [accessed 30 June 2019].

Martin, D. (1990). *Tongues of Fire: The Explosion of Protestantism in Latin America*. Oxford: Blackwell.

Marx, K., and Engels, F. [1848] (1948). *Manifesto of the Communist Party*, authorized English translation edited and annotated by Friedrich Engels. New York: International Publishers.

Mernissi, F. (1991). *The Veil and the Male Elite: A Feminist Interpretation of Women's Rights in Islam*. New York: Basic.

Mir-Hosseini, Z. (2013). Justice, Equality and Muslim Family Laws: New Ideas, New Prospects. In Z. Mir-Hosseini, Lena Larsen, Christian Moe, and Kari Vogt (eds.), *Gender and Equality in Muslim Family Law: Justice and Ethics in the Islamic Legal Process*, pp. 7–36. New York: I. B. Tauris.

Mohrmann, M. (2015). Feminist Ethics and Religious Ethics. *Journal of Religious Ethics*, 43(2): 185–192.

Momsen, J. H. (2001). Backlash: Or How to Snatch Failure from the Jaws of Success in Gender and Development. *Progress in Development Studies*, 1(1): 51–56.

Monagan, S. (2010). Patriarchy: Perpetuating the Practice of Female Genital Mutilation. *Journal of Alternative Perspectives in the Social Sciences*, 2(1): 160–181.

Paechter, C. (2006). Reconceptualising the Gendered Body: Learning and Constructing Masculinities and Feminities in School. *Gender and Education*, 18(2): 121–135.

Petersen, A. (1998). *Unmasking the Masculine: "Men" and "Identity" in a Sceptical Age*. London: Sage.

Riesebrodt, M. (2000). Fundamentalism and the Resurgence of Religion. *Numen*, 47(3): 266–287.

Sarkar, M. (2014). Feminism for Goddesses: Does Goddess Worship Empower Girls? *The Guardian. Violence Against Women: 1bn Rising Adolescent Girls – Global Development Professionals Network*. Available from: www.theguardian. com/global-development-professionals-network/2014/mar/05/india-hinduism-goddesses-feminism-global-development [accessed 23 April 2019].

Seguino, S. (2011). Help or Hindrance? Religion's Impact on Gender Inequality in Attitudes and Outcomes. *World Development*, 39(8): 1308–1321.

Sholkamy, H. (2011). Creating Conservatism in Emancipating Subjects? On the Narrative of Islamic Observance in Egypt. *IDS Bulletin*, 42(1): 47–55.

Sultana, A. (2011). Patriarchy and Women's Subordination: A Theoretical Analysis. *The Arts Faculty Journal*.

Sultana, A. (2012). Patriarchy and Women's Subordination: A Theoretical Analysis. *The Arts Faculty Journal*, (4): 1–18.

Tadros, M. (2011). Religion, Rights and Gender at the Crossroads. *IDS Bulletin*, 42(1).

Tomalin, E. (2007). *Gender Studies Approaches to the Relationships Between Religion and Development*. RaD Working Papers Series 4. Birmingham, UK: University of Birmingham.

Trzebiatowska, M., and Bruce, S. (2012). *Why Are Women More Religious Than Men?* Oxford: Oxford University Press.

Wadud, A. (1994). *Quran and Women. Journal of Islamic Studies*, pp. 324–326. Oxford: Oxford University Press.

Walby, S. (1990). *Theorizing Patriarchy*. Oxford: Blackwell.

Walter, T., and Davie, G. (1998). The Religiosity of Women in the Modern West. *The British Journal of Sociology*, 49(4): 640–660.

Wilson, A. (2000). Patriarchy: Feminist Theory. In C. Kramarae and D. Spender (eds.), *Routledge International Encyclopedia of Women: Global Women's Issues and Knowledge*, pp. 1493–97. New York: Routledge.

Wilson, E. (2017). The 'Religion or Secularism' Debate on Women's Equality Obscures the Real Problem: Patriarchy. In *Religion and Global Society*, London School of Economics and Political Science. Available from: http://blogs.lse. ac.uk/religionglobalsociety/2017/03/the-religion-or-secularism-debate-on-wom ens-equality-obscures-the-real-problem-patriarchy/ [accessed 14 October 2018].

Woodberry, R. D., and Smith, C. S. (1998). Fundamentalism et al: Conservative Protestants in America. *Annual Review of Sociology*, 24(1): 25–56.

Woodhead, L. (2007). Gender Differences in Religious Practice and Significance. In J. Beckford and J. Demerath (eds.), *The Sage Handbook of the Sociology of Religion*, pp. 550–570. London: Sage.

Woodhead, L., and Catto, R. (eds.). (2012). *Religion and Change in Modern Britain*. London: Routledge.

2 Gender in development theory and practice

This chapter traces the inclusion of gender into development think-ing, spanning the introduction of the 'women in development' (WID) approach in the 1970s, the adoption of 'gender and development' (GAD) after the 1995 Beijing Conference on Women, and the current discourse on decolonising gendered development approaches. The chapter dis-cusses the political nature of GAD and the challenges of implementing it. It critically considers the existing power balance within the wider devel-opment arena that drive and maintain feminist thought at the edge of the discourse.

The chapter also offers insights into current gender approaches and pol-icy frameworks of development organisations. It focuses specifically on the differences between theory and practice and the reasons for those gaps. Such a discussion is essential because – as this book argues – for develop-ment to appropriately address the religion–gender nexus, GAD has to be better implemented overall. In light of the data collected through interviews and in-depth document analysis, my research findings suggest that the cur-rent gender agenda is virtually religion blind in that it does not exhibit a conceptual understanding of religion's impact on gender realities in devel-oping contexts and neither considers religion as a category of analysis in its planning frameworks. I situate this claim within feminist critiques of development, which show that a dominant economic development frame-work sidetracks complex gender issues and continues to focus on women as economic instruments.

The chapter is divided into three sections. Section 1 reviews the theo-retical shift from WID to GAD. Section 2 illustrates the reality of gender approaches in practice, particularly the barriers that have inhibited a thor-ough implementation of GAD. The final section explores the possibility of a post-GAD era, highlighting calls for the decolonisation of development and more attention to intersecting inequalities.

DOI: 10.4324/9781003112549-3

From 'women in development' to 'gender and development': a conceptual shift

The emergence of the 'women in development' (WID) approach in the 1970s marked the first time the role of women in international development was recognised and discussed. Boserup's (1970) work *Women's Role in Economic Development* is widely accepted to be the first published argument for women's central position within their communities and development processes. Boserup suggested that development had largely ignored women and in some cases made their situation worse. As a result, the WID approach calls for 'greater attention to women in development policy and practice, and emphasises the need to integrate them into the development process' (Reeves and Baden, 2000: 3). Nevertheless, WID is materialistic and examines women's exclusion from development processes from an economic standpoint. It draws attention to both women's economic disadvantages as a result of being excluded from development and the economic losses of excluding women. By doing so, some have criticised the WID approach for instrumentalising women's productivity for other goals, rather than promoting gender equality as an end in itself (Rowlands, 1997: 5; Kelkar, 2005).

The exclusive focus on women is another critique of the WID approach. WID assumes that by elevating women's socio-economic roles and increasing their access to resources, employment, health, education, or other services, gender discrimination will be automatically reduced (Moser, 1993; Pearson, 2000). However, the WID approach does not address the role of men and the underlying structural reasons for gender inequality. To illustrate this difference, Moser (1993) distinguishes between 'practical' and 'strategic' gender needs in her influential work *Gender Planning and Development*. The WID approach only targets women's 'practical' needs (i.e., all immediate necessities and perceived inequalities like access to education, employment, sanitation, and healthcare). However, it does not address the strategic needs necessary for women to transform their positions within gender hierarchies (Moser, 1993: 39).

Consequently, to address WID's shortcomings, the conceptual shift from women in development (WID) to gender and development (GAD) was announced in 1995 at the Fourth World Conference on Women in Beijing. The GAD approach seeks to focus on 'the socially constructed basis of differences between men and women' (Reeves and Baden, 2000: 3) and 'emphasises the need to challenge existing gender roles and relations' to tackle inequalities more effectively (Cornwall, 1997; Reeves and Baden, 2000: 3). It argues that a focus on women in isolation means to ignore women's structural subordination to men, which is the *real* problem

(Moser, 1993: 3; Cornwall, 1997). Through an emphasis on gender relations, the conceptual shift to GAD also acknowledges the vulnerability of men and the importance of their active engagement in efforts to promote gender equality (Cornwall, 1997).

In practice, however, the GAD approach has been criticised as a change in name only. Despite the introduction of GAD, gender approaches continue to focus on women in isolation and offer materialistic solutions to their subordinated roles (see Moser, 1993; Razavi and Miller, 1995; Pearson, 2000; Cornwall, 2016). Moser (1993) posits that a likely reason for this superficial change is that some development agencies and governments consider a WID approach easier and less threatening. Transforming gender relations almost always means challenging the social status quo and thereby antagonising those in power (Silberschmidt, 1991). Limited budgets, short timeframes, political constraints, and insufficient staff training rarely allow for such comprehensive reform projects. As a result, gender has not been fully mainstreamed into development as the cross-cutting discipline that it actually is (Razavi and Miller, 1995).

Even though current gendered development frameworks offer virtually no guidelines on how to engage with the role of religion conceptually, the theoretical shift from WID to GAD could provide a space for this consideration. The shift from WID to GAD recognises the role that sociocultural factors play in constructing gender roles and shaping relations between them (Reeves and Baden, 2000: 3) while also emphasising the need to challenge these norms, roles, and relations (Moser, 1993: 3; also see Cornwall, 1997). The GAD approach could accommodate the analysis of religion in three ways:

1   Through GAD's analysis of the 'sociocultural' factors: even though this is currently a vague category, it may account for religious factors as well.
2   Through GAD's social constructionist approach: it considers how dynamic social forces, such as religion, shape gender roles and relations.
3   Through its focus on strategic needs.

Moser's (1993) distinction between 'practical' and 'strategic' needs was one of the most significant changes the GAD approach introduced to theoretical considerations of gender in development. WID responds to practical needs, like providing washing machines for women, but it does not address the intra-household gender dynamics that render care work a woman's responsibility in the first place. Likewise, increasing girls' enrolment and retainment in schools does not tackle the gender bias and inequality often perpetuated in educational curricula and textbooks. Therefore, responding to practical needs is insufficient to transform gender relations within societies. Strategic needs, in turn, are identified by women[1] themselves (Moser, 1993: 39). Strategic needs vary and are context specific but tend to centre around gender relations, divisions of labour, power, and control. Addressing these needs often entails a reform of legal rights, the introduction of equal wages, the elimination of domestic violence, the protection of women's control over their bodies, and the changing of mindsets within the larger society. Strategic needs focus on the relation between men and women in the larger society. They consider the underlying structures that perpetuate systematic inequality instead of focusing solely on the allocation of material resources to ensure women's survival and productivity. Sometimes practical and strategic needs can coincide. For example, childcare is a practical need but becomes a strategic one when it is connected to the ability to build one's career.

The analysis of religion and gender in development might be best situated within the strategic needs framework of the GAD approach. This is based on my research findings as well as the vast body of literature that demonstrates the deep structural influences of religion on gender norms and vice versa. Addressing the intersection of gender and religion entails an in-depth power analysis that would not be possible within the practical needs framework.

Gender analysis tools and 'religious blindness'

In the 1990s, shortly after the launch of the GAD approach, attempts began to mainstream gender throughout the development policy and practice arena. Specifically, the goal was to take 'account of gender issues at all stages of policy-making and programme design and implementation' (Baden and Goetz, 1998: 20). As a result, aid agencies proclaimed that gender analyses should become integral to policymaking and that gender bias needs to be avoided at all stages during the project cycle. In support of this effort, GAD scholars designed gender analysis and planning tools (see Kabeer and Subrahmanian, 1996; Moser, 1993). These tools seek to guide development practitioners in their understanding of the gender implications in a given development project setting and mainstream gender accordingly. Some tools remain closely aligned with the traditional WID approach, such as the Harvard Analytical Framework. Others are more participatory and lay the potential for a more transformative GAD approach, such as the Gender Analysis Matrix. Analysis frameworks typically do not consider the role of religion. Following is an overview of four of the main tools:

1   *The Harvard Analytical Framework (1984)*, also called the gender roles framework, was one of the earliest frameworks designed for

gender analysis. It was developed by Catherine Overholt, Mary Anderson, and Kathleen Cloud on behalf of the Harvard Institute for International Development in collaboration with the Women in Development office of the United States Agency for International Development. The framework is designed as a matrix for collecting data relating to the gender divisions of labour. It also distinguishes between access and control over resources (Overholt, 1985). However, the framework's perspective is more efficiency based than equity oriented. The framework proposes the allocation of more material resources to women to increase their productive roles. It does not consider the structural inequalities and gender hierarchies of current resource allocation processes.

2   *The Moser Framework (1980s)* was created by Caroline Moser and Caren Levy. It was part of short courses on development planning at the Development Planning Unit of the University of London. Like the Harvard Framework, it collects quantitative data on labour division as well as access and control over resources. Additionally, it draws specific attention to women's triple roles, i.e., productive, reproductive, and community activities, while highlighting the difference between practical and strategic needs of women (Moser, 1993). The Moser Framework has been criticised for focusing on gender roles rather than on gender relationships, and therefore missing the interconnectedness of men's and women's lives (Bridge, 1999).

3   *The Gender Analysis Matrix (1993)* is a participatory gender analysis tool developed by Rani Parker, as part of her work for the Save the Children Fund in the Middle East. It is used for self-awareness and identification of a group's gender differences and different impacts of development interventions on women and men (Parker, 1993). The tool examines gender across four levels (women, men, household, and community) and considers impact in four different categories (labour, time, resources, and cultural factors) (Bratiwala and Pittman, 2010, see Figure 2.1). The tool seeks to engage both men and women in a participatory discussion to explore their gender roles and relationships. It provides a certain level of flexibility by allowing each category to be adapted on a case-to-case basis. Since this is a participatory data collection tool, a strong facilitator is essential to stimulate an effective discussion of gender roles and relations (Bridge, 1999). This is the only gender analysis tool that suggests a category for 'cultural factors'. But it does not define what constitutes 'cultural'. As such, this category leaves much room for assumptions and may function as a wildcard for virtually any social influence. There is a need for development literature to clarify its use of 'culture' in relation to other social factors, such as religion, patriarchy, or tradition. A bland single category for culture

	Labour	*Time*	*Resources*	*Cultural factors*
Women				
Men				
Household				
Community				

Figure 2.1 Gender Analysis Matrix

may tempt development practitioners to uncritically accept social norms as wholly cultural and fixed without examining their intricacies, contestations, or gendered dimensions.

4   **The Social Relations Approach (1990s)** was developed by Naila Kabeer at the University of Sussex. It follows a socialist feminist perspective. Unlike the Harvard Framework and the Moser Framework, it does not focus on roles, resources, and activities, but centres around the relations between the state, market, community, and family. Kabeer describes this approach as gender transformative, as it does not only acknowledge gender-specific needs and constraints but additionally seeks to 'transform the existing gender relations in a more egalitarian direction through the redistribution of resources and responsibilities' (Kabeer, 1994: 19). As Kabeer explains, such gender redistribution is the most politically challenging policy approach, as it requires a shift of privileges from men to women and the sharing of responsibilities. While the Social Relations Approach identifies inequalities across multiple levels of society, it has been critiqued for disregarding women's individual agency to act outside of these relationships (Bratiwala and Pittman, 2010).

Some development organisations have developed their own organisational tools to understand gender dynamics. For example, the German International Aid Cooperation (GIZ) developed a simple reflective gender analysis tool to make public representation patterns of women and men explicit. These patterns are categorised according to *who* (defined by gender, age, ethnicity, etc.) and *what* (defined by activities and attitudes) they represent (see Figure 2.2). Similar to the Gender Analysis Matrix, this tool can be used to stimulate a participatory discussion and explore whether portrayals of people reinforce or challenge gender stereotypes as well as the potential impacts of these portrayals on institutional behaviour (GIZ 2001, in Jolly, 2002). The tool could help reveal the gender bias and stereotypes that have become 'internalised' and 'naturalised' in society over time (Reeler, 2007: 23). Other examples include the gender analysis tool by the Swedish

	Images: who they portray		Images: doing what activity?		Language		Reinforce or help to change gender stereotypes
	Women	*Men*	*Women*	*Men*	*Women*	*Men*	
Symbols							
Corporate image							
Murals							
Posters							
Labels							
Signs							
Graffiti							
Others							

Figure 2.2 GIZ Gender-Sensitive Organisation Tool

Source: Jolly, 2002: 27

International Development Cooperation Agency (SIDA) which provides a list of guiding principles, including recognising the difference between strategic and practical needs and the importance of considering intersectionality.

All gender analysis tools seek to paint a fuller picture of gender dynamics and their connection to development processes. A good gender analysis tool attempts to reveal and bring to the surface hidden 'repeated patterns of behaviour' (Reeler, 2007: 23). It aims to encourage a collective process of critically, consciously, and mutually re-examining 'what people have held to be true or important' and 'choosing whether to change or not, [while] seeing the consequences of either' (Reeler, 2007: 23). While some of the existing gender analysis tools promote such a process of self-awareness, at least in theory, no tool prompts practitioners to consider the impact of religious beliefs on gender norms. As a result, current gender analysis tools are basically *religion blind*. The impact of religion on GAD issues remains virtually invisible in practical analysis tools and, by extension, in development policy and programme implementation. GAD theory is missing links to the vast body of literature that engages with the intersection of religion and gender. An engagement with this literature becomes even more pressing as political religion is on the rise globally and is obsessively focusing on gender issues (Casanova, 2009). In Chapter 5 of this book, I propose a new gender analysis tool in an attempt to fill this gap.

Furthermore, there is no evidence that the frameworks that do exist in theory are in fact used in development practice. There is little data available on the actual application, practicability, or success rates of frameworks in gender planning and activities. Not one respondent in my sample could confirm that they are currently using any of the planning frameworks proposed in development theory. Some organisations developed their own frameworks and produced elaborate reports on them, but acknowledged that these tools are still not used in practice. Other organisations reported that they use multiple tools in conjunction with each other to obtain a more in-depth understanding. Nevertheless, participants interviewed from the same organisations said that in fact no framework was used in practice. Sometimes even gender staff were unaware of the existence of these frameworks or reports. When asked about this, research participants overwhelmingly argued that the frameworks were too complex and time consuming to be used in mainstream day-to-day development practice.

While bilateral agencies are the focus of this book, it is important to acknowledge that FBOs may also have developed tools for gender mainstreaming. Currently, there is little literature available concerned with gender analysis tools produced by FBOs. No FBO that was contacted as part of this research study agreed to share resources related to gender analyses. Based on my document analysis of five of the largest international FBOs (four Christian and one Islamic), no FBO provided a gender analysis tool in their reporting that specifically addressed the religion–gender nexus. All FBOs acknowledged the centrality of gender equality. Two FBOs discussed gender in relation to the organisation's religion. Only one had specific suggestions for gender analyses but it did not refer to religion. There is research needed to identify to what extent FBOs have critically engaged with the intersection of religion and gender. Such research needs to be aware of a likely skewed sample as it is considerably easier to access data of large international FBOs than grassroots FBOs on the ground that do not publish their material online or in English.

Gender in development practice: between instrumentalism, indifference, and political agendas

Today, every bilateral-aid-funded project has to meet certain gender criteria in line with the gender indicators proposed by the intergovernmental Organisation for Economic Cooperation and Development (OECD). In 2015, the OECD asked its 35-member countries to implement a government-wide strategy for gender equality to address gender stereotypes and remove implicit and explicit barriers to gender equality (OECD, 2016). This makes it virtually impossible for development projects to receive funding without addressing gender.

While development proposals include gender components on paper, project implementations often struggle in practice. For example, my document analysis found frequent uses of the expression 'gender transformative' in development reporting. Organisations use this descriptor to indicate that their projects would challenge gender dynamics. However, interviews with practitioners from the same organisations showed that approaches in practice continue to be focused on addressing practical needs and less on the transformation of gender norms. As such, organisations' use of the term gender transformative rarely aligns with theoretical conceptions of it. Kabeer (1994) distinguishes between three types of gender-aware policy: gender neutral, gender specific, and gender transformative. All three approaches acknowledge gender-specific needs and constraints, but gender-transformative approaches additionally seek to 'transform the existing gender relations in a more egalitarian direction through the redistribution of resources and responsibilities' (Kabeer, 1994: 19). These approaches are the most challenging policy approaches and the least employed ones in current bilateral development. As Moser (1993) and Silberschmidt (1991) had previously noted, any approach that shakes gendered power relations will likely be perceived as too threatening.

The gap between the acknowledgement of gender issues on paper and their translation into practice appears to be driven by 1) a preference for instrumentalist gender approaches, 2) discursive and organisational power dynamics that systematically sideline gender, and 3) political agendas of donor and recipient countries that conflict with GAD goals.

Instrumentalism: gender is used as a means to an end

Chant and Sweetman (2012: 524) have argued that '[w]omen are enlisted as foot soldiers to serve in battles whose aims are not related directly to their interests'. They critique current gender approaches for pressuring women – who often already are the main caretakers of families – to now also become entrepreneurs, economic actors, and agents of social change. Moreover, these additional responsibilities are more likely to benefit others than the women themselves. Razavi's (1997) analysis of instrumentalism in the context of GAD approaches may be one of the most influential ones. She situates this instrumentalism within the 'efficiency approach', which operates under the assumption that it makes economic sense for development aid projects to allocate resources to women since it will make development more efficient (Razavi and Miller, 1998). Development literature – explicitly or implicitly – has perpetuated this efficiency approach: for example, women have been hailed as change agents for economic growth (Duflo, 2012), fertility decline (Jones, 2007), public health and well-being (Schultz, 1995), or food security (Mehra and Rojas, 2008). This instrumentalism is reminiscent of the WID approach and promotes a development framework grounded in economically measurable outcomes with speedy, easy, and transferable solutions.

Nevertheless, instrumentalism is not always seen as something negative. In fact, some highlight the advantages of instrumentalist approaches. Olivius (2014: 11), for example, draws attention to the largely positive and active images of women it conveys. Recognising women as strategic partners and key actors in development processes is indeed an improvement to previous representations of women as passive victims with little to no agency. Nonetheless, Olivius acknowledges that instrumentalism only portrays women positively to the extent that they are perceived to be essential to aid-effectiveness. Others also point to the occasional necessity of instrumentalising women to achieve gender results. Razavi (1997) appears to be the most vocal proponent of this. She posits that the use of instrumentalism is inevitable, especially in light of working with complex gender realities on one hand and gender-hostile institutions on the other. The main challenge is to incentivise reluctant development practitioners to engage with gender in policy discussions. Her analysis has been commended by other gender and development scholars for acknowledging the struggles gender advisors encounter when addressing mainstream staff, including the 'everyday political battles and sectional interests' common in all development organisations and the 'hostility and indifference' to the subject of gender generally (Cornwall et al., 2009: 108). Razavi argues that such realities often leave internal gender advocates with little other option than instrumentalism. As Cornwall et al. (2009: 108) argue, they have to use 'whatever discursive means make sense to fight their corner', and present arguments in a way that makes them more likely to be accepted and acted upon. In such circumstances, Razavi (1997) deems criticisms of instrumentalism unhelpful.

My research identified instances of both instrumentalism as an efficient approach as well as a coping mechanism for gender advocates. However, it is difficult to distinguish the two since boundaries are blurred and often overlap. Moreover, nearly four decades of instrumentalising women have arguably normalised the practice. One only needs to look at current titles of donor policy papers to see this tendency: 'Empowering women is smart economics', 'To boost growth: Employ women', 'Change starts with a girl', or 'The economic gains of investing in girls'.

Indifference: gender considerations remain at the margin of development practice

Organisations' gender staff typically prepare gender analyses and recommendations for all divisions and workstreams of their organisation to comply with the OECD's gender mandate. However, according to my research participants, the work that gender staff provide is little used. Sometimes it is not read at all. Lisa, a gender advisor of a government aid agency, remembers the 'extreme level of disinterest' she usually encounters when proposing gender recommendations. She recalled 'testing' whether project leaders had read her recommendations and was not surprised to find that they rarely had. Jennifer, a gender advisor of a recipient organisation, similarly argued that mainstream staff considers gender relevant to their workstreams. It is considered as yet another project hurdle and box to check. They often ask 'what can gender do for us?' and 'why is this relevant to us?'.[2] The almost impossible task of incentivising mainstream staff to consider gender may then lead to the type of instrumentalist messaging Razavi described. According to my research participants, gender activities generated more interest among mainstream staff when presented as a silver bullet for other goals. Individual disinterest in gender is also mirrored in organisational structures and resource allocation, including limited gender budgets and small gender teams. Most organisations' gender teams only consisted of a handful of members. They worked separately from other staff. Assigning gender responsibilities to a few people contradicts written commitments to gender mainstreaming as chronicled in OECD guidelines and government policy. Gender staff are left carrying the burden of persuading the rest of the organisation to adopt GAD principles, often rendering instrumentalist or checklist approaches as the only feasible options. Moreover, the isolation of gender issues reinforces the idea of gender as a separate category in development rather than as a mainstreamed and cross-cutting discipline.

Political agendas: gender policies are subject to donor and recipient government policies

Gender activities not only tend to focus on economic efficiency, but they are also expected to be politically compatible and expedient for government donors. As detailed earlier, contrary to GAD's call to challenge and transform gender norms, gender practice displays a strong focus on WID-like approaches. This preference is not made explicit in policy documents[3] (which typically imply equal attention to practical and strategic gender needs) but becomes clear through interviews with practitioners. The avoidance of controversy is at odds with the very nature of gender equality reforms. As one women rights activist puts it:

> Of course, it will be controversial. Change is always a process and it's challenging. So yes, it will be controversial, but it would be controversial anywhere you go.
>
> (Nabila, women's rights activist, Malawi)

Gender and religion, each by themselves is considered a complicated issue. Subsequently, the intersection of the two finds itself at the epicentre of controversy. Most research participants felt that religion and strategic gender needs were most likely avoided because development navigates within diplomatic and political spheres and, therefore, has to be careful about how interventions are framed. Development interventions are careful to ensure political expedience and avoid upsetting countries' authorities. This is especially the case for bilateral aid which is provided by one government to another. My research identifies two political factors that appear to impact organisations' gender programming: a) bilateral aid needs political legitimacy to operate within the recipient country and b) bilateral aid is influenced by its own political religion.

Political legitimacy in recipient countries

Most research participants of government aid agencies argued that it is virtually impossible to pursue development projects or partner with organisations that the given local authority does not see as legitimate. One European government participant used the example of Indonesia. She explained that since the Ministry of Religious Affairs is very powerful in the country and influences public policymaking, development projects should therefore always consult with this ministry first on any planned intervention. On the contrary, an Indonesian women's rights activist, Nadine, argued that Western development discourses tend to 'jump to conclusion and gross simplifications' about the role of Islam in her country, especially when it comes to gender. Nadine argued that principles of gender equality are in no way new to the Indonesian contexts and, as such, should not be seen as controversial by development practitioners. Nevertheless, she doubted that foreign government officials would agree with this notion.

Political hesitance to engage with *sensitive* gender issues could be observed across all participating aid agencies. High-ranking employees of aid agencies were especially conscious of their roles as country representatives and were cautious not to drive their governments into controversy. One exception was aid given to Zimbabwe. Research participants argued that partnerships in Zimbabwe are formed even with LGBTI organisations the government does not approve of because the legitimacy of the government itself is questioned. In all other cases, aid programmes and partnerships were closely aligned with the agendas of local authorities. This can make it almost impossible to address gender beyond practical needs and challenge traditional gender regimes. One government aid agency even halted all their anti-FGM activities because the issue became 'too controversial'. The agency had already chosen a weaker approach: only address

FGM as a health issue and avoid the strategic need to challenge patriarchal gender norms that underpin the practice.

While bilateral development activities tend to shy away from the interplay of religion and gender, local women's rights activists emphasised how integral it is to engage in this space. A women's rights activist said that she was disappointed but not surprised by development's disengagement with religious laws and said:

> Western secular intellectuals and activists, they often take the position – A strategic position to not engage with religion because they believe that religion is divisive and inherently unjust and can't be changed.
>
> (Gina, women's rights activist, Egypt)

A women's rights activist in Morocco expressed similar sentiments:

> when you remain silent . . . you leave this space empty or for those who use religion to oppress women.
>
> (Salma, women's rights activist, Morocco)

The avoidance of sensitive issues not only precludes addressing strategic needs and perpetuates existing power dynamics, but it also makes it challenging to support marginalised voices of local feminist actors who seek to transform underlying structures of inequality. Nevertheless, there are exceptions to the rule. One of the government aid agencies studied during my research has supported the National Women's Rights Network in Egypt over the past decade, which seeks to reform the highly controversial family law based on feminist Islamic interpretations. Notably, all other government aid agencies have argued that it would be difficult – and perhaps unthinkable – for them to engage in such activities. It is noteworthy that the conservation of gender politics under traditional – often religious – rule was also common during the colonial era. In Egypt, for example, British colonial authorities chose to keep family matters under traditional law to symbolise cultural and religious continuity in the new political order (Tucker, 2008: 65). This made governing easier for colonial elites. The same approach was applied in India and Bangladesh, where British rule preferred to govern each religion under a separate legal code. These codes still exist today and continue to legalise gender discrimination in the name of religion. I elaborate on this in Chapter 5.

The influences of donor countries' political religion
on gender programming

Gendered political religion and the adherence to development intervention to political ideologies go both ways. That is, bilateral aid is also closely aligned to the gender discourses and debates within their own countries, which can be permeated by religious discourses. In this sense, it seems equally impossible for a bilateral aid agency to pursue a development project that its donor government does not approve of. For example, the conservative right in the United States has been pushing for an equally conservative foreign aid policy. Conservative politicians ground much of their ideology on the religious values of their core Christian constituencies, especially when it comes to gender issues. As a result, the United States has imposed restrictions on activities related to abortion or sex work and promotes a firm adherence to sexual abstinence (USAID, 2020). Based on my interviews and document analysis of over 70 donor reports, my findings indicate a consistent correlation between domestic religious discourses of Western countries and their foreign development policy. The example of the United States is well suited for this discussion since evidence for it is publicly available and can, therefore, be disclosed.

The example of the United States

The following three policy areas are examples of how internal political religion has shaped US foreign aid approaches.

Abortion

The Mexico City policy, also referred to as the global gag rule, is a US government policy that blocks federal funding for NGOs worldwide that provide abortion counselling or referrals, or advocate to decriminalise abortion (Bendavid et al., 2011). The policy was first enacted in 1984 and has since been alternately repealed and reinstated by different presidents. At times, it encompassed almost all U.S. global health aid, including organisations providing services related to HIV, malaria, and maternal and child health (Miller et al., 2019). The US government's foreign stance on abortion mirrors its ongoing domestic debates around this subject. Those, in turn, are embedded in religious debates (Gutterman and Murphy, 2016; Hirschl et al., 2012). In 2019, Trump's Protecting Life in Global Health Assistance policy expanded the gag rule restricting 'gagged' organisations not only from providing access to or information about abortion but also from engaging with organisations that do. Subsequently, even aid providers that do not accept US funding are now bound by its gender ideologies. Such restrictions have impacts beyond abortion since many organisations who became ineligible for funding are also major suppliers of contraceptives and family planning information. According to statistical studies, abortion restrictions can have unintended consequences. They can lead to less access to contraception, more unwanted pregnancies, and more abortions – many of which are likely performed unsafely (Miller et al., 2019). In 2021, the new administration rescinded the Mexico City policy (Lieberman, 2021).

Sex work

In the case of sex work, the situation is subtler. There is a growing body of literature around sex workers and how development could assist the improvement of their living conditions, for example, by providing health services, childcare, contraception, or laws that regulate social insurance (see Cornwall, 2016). However, in written reporting of the United States Agency for International Development's (USAID) (2014), sex work is commonly mentioned in direct conjunction with sex trafficking. As such, it is presented as inherently negative and harmful. While development literature acknowledges the complexities and differences between the two, the conflation of them in USAID policy renders sex work an issue of morality alone.

Abstinence

Out of the three policy domains examined here, abstinence programmes have received the most attention in development literature. US international HIV/AIDS policies have been criticised for promoting moral arguments for abstinence and empowering conservative religious voices in developing countries. In 2003 the US Congress created the President's Emergency Plan for AIDS Relief (PEPFAR) to provide 15 billion US dollars in international aid to combat HIV/AIDS primarily in Sub-Saharan Africa. The US Conference of Catholic Bishops had successfully lobbied for the insertion of a 'conscience clause' that exempted FBOs from having to 'endorse, utilize or participate in a prevention method to which the organization has a religious or moral objection' (Miller, 2014: 215). This exemption clause funded FBOs that promoted a conservative religious ideology and excluded any mention of condoms. In 2008, lobbying by US Catholic actors succeeded in delinking family planning services from HIV/AIDS prevention efforts (O'Brien, 2017).

As part of PEPFAR, Abstinence-Only-Until-Marriage (AOUM) programmes were developed. They are since prevalent in both US domestic policy and foreign aid programmes and are strongly supported by religious conservatives in the United States (Santelli, Kantor et al., 2017; Santelli, Speizer et al., 2013). Following US federal funding requirements, they systematically withhold information about human sexuality. Consequently, they have been criticised for promoting medically inaccurate information, undermining sex education, withholding life-saving information about risk reduction, promoting the practice of 'miracle cures' through charismatic faith healing, and in some instances for having the unintended consequence of encouraging early marriage (Duflo, 2012; Imam et al., 2017: 30). The introduction of the ABC (Abstinence, Be faithful, use a Condom) approach was intended to loosen the AOUM approach but research found that there was a disproportionate promotion of the A and the B over the C (Barnett and Parkhurst, 2005). International Human Rights organisations have called this 'a triumph of ideology over public health' and are hence advocating for science-based approaches (Human Rights Watch, 2003). They have called out US secondary-school materials used in Uganda for falsely stating that latex condoms have microscopic pores that can be permeated by HIV and that pre-marital sex is a form of 'deviance'. Santelli argues that the vocabulary used when addressing issues of sexuality is evident of the persisting religious elements in HIV/AIDS responses. He argues that contrary to science-based health programming which invokes terminology, such as 'vaginal sex', 'sexually active', or 'postponing sex', AOUM policies generally define abstinence in moral terms, using language, such as 'chastity', 'faithfulness', 'monogamous', and 'virgin'. Abstinence-only sex education has often created a connection between virginity and self-worth (also see van de Walle and van de Walle, 1988).

In 2002, a US executive order sought to reaffirm the separation of Church and State as per the country's constitution. It proclaimed that:

> organizations that engage in inherently religious activities, such as worship, religious instruction, and proselytization, must offer those services separately in time or location from any programs or services supported with direct Federal financial assistance.
>
> (Federal Register, 2002)

Nevertheless, AOUM approaches continue to reproduce 'Christian fundamentalist discourses' in their HIV/AIDS programmes, affecting development discourses on gender and sexuality (Imam et al., 2017: 30). Even though the danger and ineffectiveness of these programmes have been repeatedly flagged, USAID continues to defend them and has only partially loosened them (Cohen and Tate, 2006). In 2007, the Association for Women's Rights in Development (AWID) identified USAID and its AIDS Relief Plan as the 'most commonly cited specific examples of international institutional funders investing in work which supports fundamentalist visions' (Imam et al., 2017: 28 on behalf of AWID). According to Imam et al. (2017), some of the Christian groups who were empowered and legitimised through USAID Aids funding have now shifted their focus 'from abstinence campaigning to rallying homophobia'. Notably, the imposition of conservative morality and values stands in stark contrast with development's aim to appear neutral and deliver the best outcomes.

Religiously conservative gender ideologies have not only infiltrated the bilateral development aid sphere but have equally surfaced within the nonprofit realm. The 2018 report of the Global Philanthropy Project (GPP) on religious conservatism shows that religious opposition to sexuality and gender equality has spiked worldwide over the past two decades in part due to the establishment of large conservative NGOs. The report lists all religious conservative NGOs that work at the United Nations – 16 out of 17 are headquartered in the United States. These well-funded NGOs were founded in Evangelical Protestantism, Catholic, and Mormon faiths as a direct response to the UN Conferences in Cairo and Beijing in the mid-1990s.

Literature has long highlighted the United States as a unique case among Western countries in its experience of 'a religious fundamentalist movement' in the form of the 'new Christian right' (see Casanova, 1994: 135, also see Clarke, 2007). The GPP (2018: 21) report finds that:

> US politics seems to be the engine of the religious conservative activism working from the civil society in international scenarios, in a search for exporting local 'culture wars' to global arenas.

But the United States is not the only Western country that has experienced a surge in right-wing Christian voices within politics that influence – or at least seek to influence – foreign aid strategies. My research data indicates that the same argument could easily be constructed for many other countries in the West. For instance, Europe's rise in public religion merits renewed attention. Nevertheless, given the US' dominant role in the global development sector and its influential religious political right, a conversation about religious pushbacks on gender equality must include the US foreign aid policy and how it restricts sexual and reproductive health rights (SRHRs) worldwide and emboldens grassroots anti-choice initiatives. Any internal political changes within the United States are likely to be impactful globally. One of the most recent examples may be the United States' obstruction of a UN resolution providing reproductive health services for rape victims in conflict zones (Opal, 2019).

Moving towards a post-GAD era: decolonising development and addressing intersectional inequalities

The export of cultural values and gender ideologies as part of development projects has been called out by postcolonial and decolonial development critiques. Much of this critique is influenced by Foucault's work on power and knowledge, as well as Edward Said's work *'Orientalism'*. Spivak (1993) uses Foucault's term 'epistemic violence' to describe the destruction of non-Western worldviews and the resulting epistemological hegemony of Western knowledge. This hegemony is produced by what Jordan (1997) calls authoritative knowledge. Following Foucault's theory of power and knowledge, Jordan argues that authoritative knowledge means that one form of knowledge gains ascendance and legitimacy over another. In other words, authoritative knowledge is the knowledge that *counts* in a given place, it dictates the decisions that are made and the actions that are taken. In the US example, this authoritative knowledge lies with the Christian right.

During the colonial period, authoritative knowledge and cultural hegemony were frequently justified by orientalist arguments. These consisted of the depiction of non-Western societies as simplistic, uncivilised, and backwards. In conjunction with political power, such orientalist portrayals became crucial in administering and subjugating colonies (Said, 1978). Postcolonial development critiques have drawn attention to the long-lasting consequences and cultural legacy of colonialism. They also argue that current development can be understood as a continuation of colonial domination. Today, most Western government-backed development efforts continue to be closely aligned with the economic and political agenda of the sponsoring government. Omar (2012), based on Said's (1978) arguments, describes development as yet another style of Western knowledge designed for dominating, restructuring, and controlling the 'underdeveloped world'. Similarly, Escobar (2007), who draws on Said and Foucault, calls out Western development's convenient discovery of poverty to reassert its moral and cultural superiority in supposedly postcolonial times. Kothari (2005: 47) has also criticised the sector for ignoring its colonial roots and continuing to produce knowledge in deeply hierarchical patterns.

As a result of postcolonial development critique, calls for decolonising development have become louder over the past decade. Scholars and activists are demanding a revision of current one-way development policies that do not recognise the overlapping histories and social forces of so-called developing and developed countries. Decolonising development must entail an honest conversation about hegemonic power dynamics and knowledge production. This conversation must begin with a critical reflection on how the story of development is told. As Rutazibwa (2017) suggests: do we start telling the story of development as a post-World War II project and generous gift from the West to the rest? Or do we start with transatlantic slavery and colonialism, which explains the extreme inequality between the Global North and South in the first place? Rutazibwa argues that the first version of the story presents the emergence of development in a historical vacuum assuming that so-called developing countries appeared out of nowhere. She calls on development discourses to portray Western actors not only as the 'firefighters' but also as the 'arsonists'. This would correctly implicate the West from the start of the development story. Indeed, what Western countries spend on aid today is a minuscule fraction compared to what they extracted from countries under colonial rule. For example, Britain spends about 18 million US dollars annually on overseas aid but drained 17 times as much from one of their former colonies alone: drawing on nearly two centuries of detailed data on tax and trade, new research calculated that Britain stole approximately 45 trillion US dollars from India between 1765 and 1938 (Chakrabarti and Patnaik, 2018). Strikingly, Britain appears to be neglecting all such colonial crimes. British schools are yet to include the country's colonial history in the national compulsory curriculum. Telling the story right and acknowledging the full extent of colonial rule is the first step for a meaningful process of decolonisation.

Just like education must be decolonised, development research methods and knowledge production also need a critical review to enable non-hegemonic viewpoints, approaches, and voices to enter development thinking. Omar (2008) suggests a 'mutually negotiated and collectively implemented process' based on 'ethical guidelines defined on the basis of social justice'. He redirects the primary focus of development interventions to the lived realities, concerns, and needs of beneficiaries. One of the most powerful and influential cases for beneficiaries was made in Sen's (1999) book *Development as Freedom*. Sen emphasises the need for individuals to restore their capacity to take charge of their own lives, create their own systems of existence, and participate in their autonomy. More recently, Horn (2020: 85) has advocated for a decolonial feminist approach that puts voices in the Global South at the centre of new knowledge production. Her research challenges the presumption that Western knowledge can offer the most appropriate frameworks for understanding and designing mental health interventions targeted at African women and instead draws attention to the efforts of African feminists.

Decolonising development is especially important for GAD approaches because colonialism itself was deeply gendered (Cornwall, 2017). Gendered development approaches must recognise their colonial roots to avoid repeating gender stereotypes and orientalist depictions of women and men. Today's development aid continues to impose ideological values through its gender programming. Meanwhile, it continues to ignore or misconstrue the dynamic intersection of religion and gender in their own and recipient countries. Abu-Lughod (2002) warns that simplified representations of religious women can have dangerous effects. For example, the portrayal of Muslim women as oppressed served as justifications for the War on Terror and America's invasion of Afghanistan while simultaneously covering up messy historical and political dynamics that have perpetuated inequality (Abu-Lughod, 2002; Stabile and Kumar, 2005). Development policies, especially bilateral aid, are situated within the same political sphere and, as such, equally susceptible to prevalent Western-centric notions of gender and religion.

Traditional WID approaches that instrumentalise women and view them as 'object(s) of rescue' or 'vulnerable, virtuous victims' with no agency are similar to the way Western colonial empires treated women (Cornwall, 2017). Additionally, Cornwall explains that many Western gender ideals were imported and imposed on colonies, such as the idea of a gender binary, heteronormativity, and even the nuclear household. Cornwall argues that these all stem from Western Christian ideas about sex and intrude on local cultural norms around the globe. She mentions several consequences of this. For example, by adhering to the colonial emphasis on nuclear households, contemporary development approaches have adopted households as units of analysis. Nevertheless, this obscures gendered power dynamics within households. A different consequence is the erasing of third genders in some countries by colonial gender ideologies. For example, third genders were common in the Hindu religious tradition until the arrival of British colonial authorities. But British officials described third genders as connected to 'filth, disease, contagion and contamination' (Biswas, 2019). They were considered not only 'ungovernable' and a danger to 'public morals', but also a 'threat to colonial political authority' (ibid, 2019). As such, colonialism severely marginalised local expressions that described plural forms of gender. British colonial interference in India resembles the case of Egypt illustrated earlier. These examples stress the link between decolonisation efforts and gender issues. Cornwall (2017) thus concludes that development needs:

> a renewed focus on the processes of unlearning and critical consciousness building that makes the injuries of the colonial patriarchal and heteronormativity visible, and recognition of those who are marginalised because of it.

This means that it is not enough to focus on the 'other' and 'their empowerment' but to realise one's own role in 'the encroachment on their lives' and the shaping of the narratives about them (Cornwall, 2017). Cornwall calls for the reconsideration of knowledge and assumptions, the challenging of institutions and ideas, and the reallocation of resources in development practice. If anything, current aid policy indicates that development is far from decolonisation. Political agendas continuously take priority over gender and development goals. Twenty-five years after the Beijing Conference on Women, this is a truly lamentable state of affairs.

Calls to decolonise GAD have gone hand in hand with calls to consider the 'intersectionality' of gender inequality. As detailed earlier, current gender analyses are often conducted by quick desk research and without field interviews or reference to theoretical analysis frameworks. Rushed gender analyses are prone to overlook the messiness of gender dynamics, specifically, their intersectionality. Intersectionality is the idea that inequality, discrimination, and oppression do not simply exist between two internally homogenous groups, men and women, but are experienced differently across multiple levels of social identities, such as ethnicity, age, marital status, gender identity, or sexual orientation (Crenshaw, 1991). For instance, a divorced black Muslim woman would likely face different challenges in life than an elderly married Hindu woman living in the same village. A consideration of intersectionality provides a more nuanced picture of complex gender inequalities (Yuval-Davis, 2011). The idea of 'intersecting inequalities' has been adopted by development theory over the past decade (see Kabeer, 2010). Development research has drawn attention to the double and triple disadvantages some people face based on their identity. For example, a 2015 study on Ethiopia finds that Somali girls living in rural areas only have a 15% chance of finishing school, compared to 77% of girls from other ethnicities living in urban areas (Lenhardt and Samman, 2015). In 2020, large development agencies such as UN Women (2020) have also engaged with the idea of intersecting inequalities. This idea has in fact become the underlying premise of the 2030 development agenda 'Leave No One Behind' which focuses on inclusive development. It remains to be seen how organisations will translate this agenda into practice and address the hurdles that have so far kept GAD approaches from launching successfully.

Conclusion

Current gender approaches in practice are far from the feminist intent that originally inspired them. Instrumentalist WID approaches prevail and treat women in close relation to their traditional roles. Rather than seeking to transform these roles, instrumentalist gender approaches tend to further naturalise and reaffirm existing gender inequalities and gender norms. Since I place the religion–gender nexus within GAD's strategic needs framework, I argue that a move beyond practical needs and WID approaches in development practice becomes crucial for religion to be considered at all. Until then, the role religion plays in shaping gender roles and relations is likely to continue to go unnoticed.

The shift from WID to GAD is incomplete. GAD not only needs to be better implemented but it must also undergo critical review. Decolonialisation discourses reframe development as a global project. They highlight the shared experience of high- and low-income countries and seek to even the playing field, allowing marginalised voices to become the centre of development. This was one of the key calls from the Beijing conference 25 years ago and may pave the way for understanding the religion–gender nexus as a global phenomenon.

Notes

1 While Moser developed her framework in relation to women, it should equally apply to men who may find themselves subordinated in other social contexts and have both practical and strategic needs.
2 My research found evidence of high levels of personal reluctance to development's gender agenda, which I discuss in more detail in Chapter 6.
3 Several development interventions actually claim to have addressed gender norms. Haider's (2017) work offers a comprehensive review of such interventions. The report does not specify religion. Perhaps surprisingly, none of the interventions reviewed by Haider were mentioned by the participants in my sample, despite the fact that many of them were representatives of organisations reviewed in the report. This again highlights the disconnect between development theory and gender practice.

Bibliography

Abu-Lughod, L. (2002). Do Muslim Women Really Need Saving? Anthropological Reflections on Cultural Relativism and Its Others. *American Anthropologist*, 104(3): 783–790.
Baden, S., and Goetz, A. (1998). Who Needs [Sex] When You Can Have [Gender]? In C. Jackson and R. Pearson (eds.), *Feminist Visions of Development*. London: Routledge.
Barnett, T., and Parkhurst, J. (2005). HIV/AIDS: Sex, Abstinence, and Behaviour Change. *The Lancet Infectious Diseases*, 5(9): 590–593.
Bendavid, E., Avila, P., and Miller, G. (2011). United States Aid Policy and Induced Abortion in Sub-Saharan Africa. *Geneva: Bulletin World Health Organ*, 89: 873–80.
Biswas, S. (2019). How Britain Tried to 'Erase' India's Third Gender. *BBC News*. Available from: www.bbc.com/news/world-asia-india-48442934 [accessed 29 September 2020].
Boserup, E. (1970). *Women's Role in Economic Development*. London: George Allen & Unwin.
Bratiwala, S., and Pittman, A. (2010). *Capturing Change in Women's Realities a Critical Overview of Current Monitoring and Evaluation Frameworks*. Toronto:

AWID. Available from: http://brookeackerly.org/wp-content/uploads/2010/11/Batliwala-2010.pdf [accessed 1 September 2019].

Bridge. (1999). *Gender Planning Frameworks*. Brighton: University of Sussex, Institute of Development Studies. Available from: www.bridge.ids.ac.uk/sites/bridge.ids.ac.uk/files/docs_gem/index_implementation/pf_coretext.htm [accessed 1 September 2017].

Casanova, J. (1994). *Public Religions in the Modern World*. Chicago: The University of Chicago Press.

Casanova, J. (2009). Religion, Politics and Gender Equality: Public Religions Revisited. In S. Razavi (ed.), *A Debate on the Public Role of Religion and Its Social and Gender Implications*. Geneva: UN Research Institute for Social Development, Gender and Development Programme Paper No. 5.

Chakrabarti, S., and Patnaik, U. (eds.). (2018). *Agrarian and Other Histories: Essays for Binay Bhushan Chaudhuri*. New Delhi: Tulika Books.

Chant, S., and Sweetman, C. (2012). *Fixing Women or Fixing the World?* Smart Economics, Efficiency Approaches and Gender Equality. Development. *Gender and Development*, 20(3): 517–529.

Clarke, G. (2007). Agents of Transformation? Donors, Faith-Based Organisations and International Development. *Third World Quarterly*, 28(1): 77–96.

Cohen, J., and Tate, T. (2006). The Less They Know, the Better: Abstinence-Only HIV/AIDS Programs in Uganda. *Reproductive Health Matters*, 14(28): 174–178.

Cornwall, A. (1997). Men, Masculinities and 'Gender in Development'. *Gender and Development*, 5(2): 8–13. Taylor & Francis, Ltd. on behalf of Oxfam GB.

Cornwall, A. (2016). Women's Empowerment: What Works? *Journal of International Development*, 28: 342–359.

Cornwall, A. (2017). *Decolonising Gender and Development*. Lecture. Institute of Development Studies. Available from: www.ids.ac.uk/events/decolonising-gender-and-development/ [accessed 19 October 2020].

Cornwall, A., Harrison, E., and Whitehead, A. (eds.). (2009). *Feminisms in Development: Contradictions, Contestations and Challenges*. London: Zed Books.

Crenshaw, K. (1991). Mapping the Margins: Intersectionality, Identity Politics, and Violence Against Women of Color. *Stanford Law Review*, 43(6): 1241–1299.

Duflo, E. (2012). Women Empowerment and Economic Development. *Journal of Economic Literature*, 50(4): 1051–1079.

Escobar, A. (2007). Worlds and Knowledges Otherwise. *Cultural Studies*, 21(2–3): 179–210.

Federal Register. (2002). Executive Order 13279 – Equal Protection of the Laws for Faith-Based and Community Organizations. *Federal Register*, 67(241). Available from: www.federalregister.gov/documents/2002/12/16/02-31831/equal-protection-of-the-laws-for-faith-based-and-community-organizations [accessed 28 July 2020].

GPP. (2018). Religious Conservatism on the Global Stage: Threats and Challenges for LGBTI Rights. *Global Philanthropy Project*. Available from: https://globalphilanthropyproject.org/religiousconservatismreport/ [accessed 19 September 2020].

Gutterman, D. S., and Murphy, A. R. (2016). *Political Religion and Religious Politics: Navigating Identities in the United States*. New York: Routledge.

Haider, H. (2017). Changing Gender and Social Norms, Attitudes and Behaviours. Knowledge, Evidence and Learning for Development. *K4D Helpdesk Report*. University of Birmingham. Available from: www.gsdrc.org/wp-content/uploads/2017/05/K4D_HDQ89.pdf [accessed 23 May 2019].

Hirschl, T. A., Booth, J. G., Glenna, L. L., and Green, B. Q. (2012). Politics, Religion, and Society: Is the United States Experiencing a Period of Religious-Political Polarization? *Review of European Studies*, 4(4): 95–109.

Horn, J. (2020). Decolonising Emotional Well-Being and Mental Health in Development: African Feminist Innovations. *Gender & Development*, 28(1): 85–98.

Human Rights Watch (2003). *Policy Paralysis: A Call for Action on HIV/AIDS-related Human Rights Abuses against Women and Girls in Africa*. Available from: https://www.hrw.org/sites/default/files/reports/africa1203.pdf [accessed 15 November 2019].

Imam, A., Gokal, S., and Marler, I. (2017). The Devil is in the Details: A Feminist Perspective on Development, Women's Rights, and Fundamentalisms. *Gender and Development*, 25(1): 15–36.

Jolly, S. (2002). *Gender and Cultural Change. Supporting Resources Collection*. Brighton: University of Sussex, Institute of Development Studies, BRIDGE.

Jones, G. W. (2007). Fertility Decline in Asia: The Role of Marriage Change. *Asia-Pacific Population Journal*, 22(2): 13–32.

Jordan, B. (1997). *Birth in Four Cultures: A Cross-Cultural Investigation of Childbirth in Yucatan, Holland, Sweden, and the United States*. 4th Ed. Prospect Heights, IL: Waveland Press Inc.

Kabeer, N. (1994). *Reversed Realities: Gender Hierarchies in Development Thought*. London: Verso Press.

Kabeer, N. (2010). *Can the MDGs Provide a Pathway to Social Justice? The Challenge of Intersecting Inequalities*. New York: United Nation Development Programme.

Kabeer, N., and Subrahmanian, R. (1996). Institutions, Relations and Outcomes: A Framework and Tools for Gender-Aware Planning. *IDS Discussion Paper* No. 357, Brighton: IDS.

Kelkar, G. (2005). Development Effectiveness Through Gender Mainstreaming: Gender Equality and Poverty Reduction in South Asia. *Economic and Political Weekly*, 40(44/45): 4690–4699.

Kothari, U. (2005). A Radical History of Development Studies: Individuals, Institutions and Ideologies. In U. Kothari (ed.), *A Radical History of Development Studies*. London: Zed Books.

Lenhardt, A., and Samman, E. (2015). In Quest of Inclusive Progress: Exploring Intersecting Inequalities in Human Development. *Development Progress Research Report*, 4. Climate and Development Knowledge Network and Overseas Development Institute: London.

Lieberman, A. (2021). *Biden Repeals the 'Global GAG Rule,' But Next Steps Will Be Huge Undertaking'*. Inside Development, Devex: Washington, DC. Available

48   *Why the religion–gender nexus matters*

from: www.devex.com/news/biden-repeals-the-global-gag-rule-but-next-steps-will-be-huge-undertaking-98954 [accessed 28 April 2021].

Mehra, R., and Rojas, M. H. (2008). *Women, Food Security and Agriculture in a Global Marketplace*. Washington, DC: International Center for Research on Women (ICRW).

Miller, P. (2014). *Good Catholics: The Battle Over Abortion in the Catholic Church*. Berkeley, CA: University of California Press.

Miller, G., Bendavid, E., and Brooks, N. (2019). *How US Government Restrictions on Foreign Aid for Abortion Services Backfired. Institute for Economic Policy Research*. Palo Alto: Stanford University.

Moser, C. (1993). *Gender Planning and Development: Theory, Practice and Training*. London: Routledge.

O'Brien, J. (2017). Can Faith and Freedom Co-Exist? When Faith-Based Health Providers and Women's Needs Clash. *Gender & Development*, 25(1): 37–51.

OECD. (2016). *2015 OECD Recommendation of the Council on Gender Equality in Public Life*. Paris: OECD Publishing.

Olivius, E. (2014). *Three Approaches to Gender in Humanitarian Aid. Department of Political Science and Umea for Gender Studies*. Sweden: Umea.

Omar, S. (2012). Rethinking Development from a Postcolonial Perspective. *Journal of Conflictology*, 3(1).

Opal, J. M. (2019). U.S. Obstructs UN Resolution on Rape. Why? A Long History of Religious Nationalism. *The Conversation*. Available from: https://theconversation.com/u-s-obstructs-un-resolution-on-rape-why-a-long-history-of-religious-nationalism-116105 [accessed 5 May 2019].

Overholt, C., Anderson, M. B., Cloud, K., and Austin, J. E. (eds.). (1985). *Gender Roles in Development Projects: A Case Book*. West Hartford, CT: Kumarian Press.

Parker, R. (1993). *Another Point of View: A Manual on Gender Analysis Training for Grassroots Workers*. New York: UNIFEM.

Pearson, R. (2000). Rethinking Gender Matters in Development. In T. Allen and A. Thomas (eds.), *Poverty and Development into the 21st Century*, pp. 383–402. Milton Keynes: Open University in Association with Oxford University Press.

Razavi, S. (1997). Fitting Gender into Development Institutions. *World Development*, 25(7): 1111–1125.

Razavi, S., and Miller, C. (1995). *From WID to GAD: Conceptual Shifts in the Women and Development Discourse*. UNRISD Occasional Paper, no. 1, Geneva.

Reeler, D. [2007] (2016). *A Three-fold Theory of Social Change – and Implications for Practice, Planning, Monitoring and Evaluation*. Cape Town: Centre for Developmental Practice CDRA. Available from: www.cdra.org.za/uploads/1/1/1/6/111664/threefold_theory_of_change_-_and_implications_for_pme_-_doug_reeler_of_the_cdra.pdf [accessed 28 March 2018].

Reeves, H., and Baden, S. (2000). *Gender and Development: Concepts and Definitions*. Prepared for the Department for International Development (DFID) for Its Gender Mainstreaming Intranet Resource. Report No. 55. Brighton: University of Sussex, Institute of Development Studies, BRIDGE. Available from: www.bridge.ids.ac.uk/reports/re55.pdf [accessed 27 August 2019].

Rowlands, J. (1997). *Questioning Empowerment: Working with Women in Hondu-ras.* London: Oxfam.

Rutazibwa, O. (2017). *On Babies and Bathwater: Decolonising International Development Studies.* Brighton: University of Sussex, Institute of Development Studies. Available from: www.ids.ac.uk/events/on-babies-and-bathwater-decolo nising-international-development-studies/ [accessed 27 October 2020].

Said, E. W. (1978). *Orientalism.* New York: Pantheon Books.

Santelli, J. S., Kantor, L., Grilo, S. et al. (2017). *Abstinence-Only-Until-Marriage: An Updated Review of U.S. Policies and Programs and Their Impact.* Journal of Adolescent Health, 273–280.

Santelli, J. S., Speizer, I. S., and Edelstein, Z. R. (2013). Abstinence Promotion Under PEPFAR: The Shifting Focus of HIV Prevention for Youth. *Global Public Health,* 8(1): 1–12.

Schultz, T. P. (1995). *Investment in Women's Human Capital.* Chicago: University of Chicago Press.

Sen, A. (1999). *Development as Freedom.* Oxford. Oxford University Press.

Silberschmidt, M. (1991). *Rethinking Men and Gender Relations. An Investigation of Men, Their Changing Roles Within the Household, and the Implications for Gender Relations in Kisii District, Kenya.* CDR Research Report. No.16. Copenhagen.

Spivak, G. C. (1993). *Can the Subaltern Speak?* In P. Williams and L. Chrisman (eds.), *Colonial Discourse and Postcolonial Theory.* New York: Harvester Wheatsheaf.

Stabile, C. A., and Kumar, D. (2005). Unveiling Imperialism: Media, Gender and the War on Afghanistan. *Media, Culture & Society,* 27(5): 765–782.

Tucker, J. E. (2008). *Women, Family, and Gender in Islamic Law.* Cambridge: Cambridge University Press.

UN Women. (2020). Intersectional Feminism: What It Means and Why It Matters Right Now. Available from: www.unwomen.org/en/news/stories/2020/6/ explainer-intersectional-feminism-what-it-means-and-why-it-matters [accessed 28 October 2020].

USAID. (2014). *AAPD 14–04.* Washington, DC: USAID. Available from: www. usaid.gov/work-usaid/aapds-cibs/aapd-14-04 [accessed 22 October 2020].

USAID. (2020). *Global Health Legislative and Policy Requirements.* Washington, DC: USAID. Available from: www.usaid.gov/global-health/legislative-policy-requirements [accessed 22 October 2020].

Van de Walle, E., and van de Walle, F. (1988). Birthspacing and Abstinence in Sub-Saharan Africa. *International Family Planning Perspectives,* 14(1): 25–26.

Yuval-Davis, N. (2011). *The Politics of Belonging: Intersectional Contestations.* London: Sage.

3 Religion in development and its impact on gender issues

This chapter reviews the four main ways in which religion and development have crossed paths:

1 Religious institutions' histories of providing welfare, humanitarian assistance, and social services.
2 Religious actors' contributions and oppositions to the gender goals of the Beijing Platform for Action over the past 25 years.
3 Development's relationship with religion spanning Christianity-infused colonial missions, a secular post-war era, and a recent turn to religious partners.
4 Development's current religious partnerships and their potential negative gender impacts.

Religion's historic role in welfare and humanitarian aid

Religious institutions and faith-based aid are some of the oldest providers of welfare, social services, humanitarian assistance, and advocacy for social justice reform around the globe. Religions' struggle against inequality and poverty is rooted in deeply held social justice principles that can be found across religious traditions. Prominent examples include the Islamic practice of *Zakat*, the 2.5% every Muslim is required to give to those in need each year of their annual wealth. In addition to that, Muslims are obliged to care for widows and orphans and to offer protection to people of all religions fleeing conflict and persecution (Deacon and Tomalin, 2015). Other examples include Indic religions, specifically Hinduism, Sikhism, and Buddhism, which require followers to exercise *Dana* (selfless giving) and *Seva* (service) as individual duties. In Christian contexts, the Church has been a major provider of charity, shelter, and social services. In the Middle Ages hospitals were often run by the Churches and Monasteries as a result of Christianity's call to follow Jesus's example in helping the poor

DOI: 10.4324/9781003112549-4

and reducing their suffering (Ferris, 2005). Churches provided a home for those too handicapped or elderly to work, gave alms to the poor, and had guest houses for travellers and infirmaries for the sick.

Nowadays, faith-based organisations (FBOs) provide a platform for communities to exercise their religious charity duties; for instance, donations to people in need are now frequently made through FBOs rather than direct giving. With funds received, FBOs undertake a series of activities to assist the poor and work towards social justice and equality.

Religious actors and the advancement or hindrance of gender equality

Throughout history, religions have inspired both patriarchal and emancipatory social changes. Over the past 25 years, religious actors have strengthened but also hindered the achievement of the 1995 Beijing Platform for Action and later, the United Nations Sustainable Development Goal 5 (SDG 5). In the following, a brief snapshot is provided of how religious actors have advanced and delayed gender-related development goals, specifically the five targets under the SDG 5:

- end discrimination against women and girls;
- end gender-based violence (GBV);
- end child, early, and forced marriage (CEFM) and female genital mutilation (FGM);
- recognise the value of unpaid care and domestic work (UCDW);
- increase women's participation and leadership in decision-making;
- ensure sexual and reproductive health rights (SRHRs) and access.

The evidence listed here is from a recent PaRD-JLI development report that explored the dynamic, diverse, and ongoing ways in which religious actors have interpreted and addressed gender issues (Khalaf-Elledge, 2021). The examples listed are not exhaustive.

End discrimination against women and girls: In 1979, the United Nations General Assembly adopted the 'Convention on the Elimination of all Forms of Discrimination Against Women' (CEDAW). It was instituted in 1981 and has been ratified by 189 states. Six have yet to ratify it: the United States, Iran, Somalia, Sudan, Palau, and Tonga. Despite the adoption of CEDAW, many countries continue to have laws that declare husbands head of the household and sanction marital rape, wife battering, and/or honour killings. Many national governments maintain religious reservations to CEDAW articles, such as Bangladesh and Egypt. Others, such as the Philippines and Lebanon, have ratified CEDAW but still have gender-discriminatory legislation, which is protected and promoted by the national religious authority. Religious feminist movements have been pivotal in successfully campaigning for reforms of discriminatory religious family laws, such as in Egypt, India, Morocco, and Pakistan.

End gender-based violence (GBV): Religious actors have participated in local and international efforts to raise awareness about the prevalence and consequences of gender-based violence. For example, in South Africa and Thailand, religious actors have used religious teachings and texts to highlight the negative impacts of GBV and the divide between their 'true' religion and patriarchal interpretations of it. On the other hand, religious actors continue to condone GBV. For example, *marry-your-rapist* laws still exist in many countries, most recently the cases of Jordan and Lebanon made international news headlines. These laws are often protected by religious authorities based on the belief that they prevent the social stigma of premarital sex. Violence against LGBTI people is also still widespread globally and often sanctioned by religious arguments.

End child, early, and forced marriage (CEFM) and female genital mutilation (FGM): Religious leaders have publicly spoken out against child marriage and encouraged other religious actors to preach about its prevention to their congregations, for example, in India, Somalia, or Ethiopia. In Tanzania, religious leaders have come together to collectively announce their commitment to ending FGM. Somali and Mauritanian Islamic scholars have issued fatwas (i.e., religious legal opinions) banning the practice. In some countries, however, such as Egypt and Somalia, politicians continue to endorse FGM, in fear of losing votes of constituencies who continue to believe the practice is religious. Some religious leaders also continue to resist government regulations of legal marriage age since they view early marriage inherently connected to their beliefs and societal structures.

Recognise the value of unpaid care and domestic work (UCDW): Collaborations between international and grassroots organisations, for example, in Sri Lanka, Zimbabwe, and the Philippines have discussed the negative impacts of UCDW, explored the benefits of shared care responsibilities for the whole community, and promoted positive messages from religious scriptures on involved and nonviolent fatherhood. At the same time, many religious actors continue to defend traditional divisions of labour that they view as God-ordained and that keep women in domestic roles and men in public positions.

Increase women's participation and leadership in decision-making: There is limited evidence of how religious actors may have contributed to this goal. Some grassroots actors have embraced religious interpretations that encourage female participation, for example, in South Africa, Nigeria, and

Lebanon. In some countries, including Lebanon or Egypt, political parties have actively restricted women's participation.

Ensure sexual and reproductive health rights (SRHRs) and access: In many countries, religious actors can provide crucial health services due to their extensive networks and infrastructure. They have played an integral part in achieving efforts related to SRHRs, especially by combating religious misconceptions around contraception and family planning (e.g., Afghanistan, Bangladesh, Uganda, Kenya, and Senegal), by lifting the taboo around discussing these issues (e.g., Afghanistan and Bangladesh), by offering HIV counselling service (e.g., Tanzania and Nigeria) and by advocating for a change in national laws (e.g., Argentina). Meanwhile, across the globe, SRHRs continue to be a contentious subject among conservative religious actors and communities. In some countries, such as the Philippines, Malawi, Kenya, Uganda, and the United States, conservative religious forces have made efforts to restrict women's access to appropriate sexual and reproductive health services and information. Some development aid policies have emboldened and funded many such initiatives.

Development's relationship with religion: between cultural imperialism, secularism, and religious partnerships

Religion in the colonial pre-development era: Western colonialism was deeply influenced by a pervasive Christian discourse that promoted the saving of less-developed social groups (see Fiddian-Qasmiyeh, 2015). It believed that those social groups depended on external interventions and protection to develop at all (Ferris, 2011). Infused by a sense of superiority over *the Other*, colonial-cum-development systematically dismissed and cast aside other cultures and religious beliefs (Said, 2003). It forged a hierarchical separation between *us* in the West and *them*, the rest: while *we* were enlightened and developed, *they* were backwards (Volpp, 2001). The colonial process of othering has been particularly criticised for its orientalist and intrinsically gendered nature (Said, 2003; Volpp, 2001; Spivak, 1993). Volpp argues that the subordination of women was described by colonial missions to be integral only to certain non-Western societies. While women were commonly described as weak, passive, and victims, men were described as perpetrators, oppressors, and even barbaric. Spivak suggests that colonial views ultimately promoted 'saving brown women from brown men' and their oppressive cultures and religions (Spivak, 1993: 93; also see Abu-Lughod, 2013; Fiddian-Qasmiyeh, 2015). This view was particularly prominent among Christian missionary interventions supporting Western colonialism. Subsequently, these interventions centred around the so-called 'liberation' of women and children, including anti-*sati* campaigns ('widow immolation'), the unveiling of Muslim women, and forced adoption or internment programmes for so-called 'illegitimate' children (Fiddian-Qasmiyeh, 2015: 562).

Religion during the post-war development era: While during colonial-cum-development a religious Christian discourse was pervasive, the postwar newly institutionalised development industry pronounced secularism as the main driver of socio-economic progress and good governance (Fiddian-Qasmiyeh, 2015). This presumptuous declaration has arguably led to the decades-long negligence of religion's role in development.

During the 1960s and 1970s, ideas of development were very similar to ideas of the modernisation theory. The overall assumption was that all nations could reach a modern standard of living if correct policies were implemented (Mckay, 2004: 45). Development was largely associated with concepts, such as economic growth, prosperity, and progress. These ideas were soon contested by dependency theory, which argues that underdevelopment must persist in some areas to sustain development in others (i.e., rich countries rely on the exploitation of the underdeveloped world as this is how they achieve growth) (McKay, 2004: 55). In the 1980s, the 'neoliberal' ideology entered the development discourse, promoting a global deregulated market society. In other words, neoliberalism believes that capitalism will generate development and therefore insist that low-income countries remove obstacles to free market capitalism. Neoliberals also opposed any mitigating factors for developing countries debt in the 1980s and instead called for structural adjustment policies. These programmes, implemented by the International Monetary Fund (IMF), tended to use developing countries' existing debt as a lever for introducing more market-oriented reforms, even at the expense of national sovereignty (Reid-Henry, 2012).

Towards the end of the 20th century, contemporary development scholars started to challenge traditional development theories, specifically because of adverse effects of interventions such as the IMF's structural adjustment programmes. Development theorists advocated for the active involvement of the civil society of an investee country in setting objectives and methods (McKay, 2004: 63). Holistic development theories emerged and emphasised the need to focus on human capabilities and moral practices (see Sen, 1985; Nussbaum, 2011). These theories encouraged a new focus on freedom, happiness, social equality, as well as a balance between materialistic and non-materialistic factors when evaluating human welfare. Being human-centred, the capability approach prioritises what people value and calls on development interventions to correspond with such values. Presently, however, the capability approach has not yet permeated development policy or practice.

If it was to be implemented, it may open the door for considering religion as a dimension of development while recognising its centrality in people's lives and how it has long influenced welfare provision and social change. Nevertheless, Sen himself may be reluctant to grant religion such a key role within developing processes as to its 'association with identity-based conflict and violence' (Deneulin and Rakodi, 2011: 48; Sen, 2006). Around this time the concept of cultural relativism became popular (Bell et al., 2001). The idea behind the term 'cultural relativism' was first introduced by anthropologist Boas in 1887 when he wrote that 'civilization is not something absolute, but . . . relative, and . . . our ideas and conceptions are true only so far as our civilization goes' (Boas, 1887: 589). The concept itself was later coined by social theorist Locke in 1924 and became commonly used by anthropologist post-World War II. In development discourses, it operates on the following notion: when there is a difference between internal and external judgements of a norm or practice, priority should be given to the internal judgements of the society. For example, Goulet (1980) suggested that development should define its goals in line with the value system of respective communities as it will strengthen development's programme design and outcomes. However, a key risk has been that development practitioners and scholars have treated culture 'in the totalizing, undifferentiated way in which some leaders of non-Western nations have used it as a trump card' to justify harmful practices or the crushing of political dissent (Bell et al., 2001: 21). Practices *protected* by cultural relativism tend to be the most controversial – often untouched – challenges within the gender domain of development, for example, forced marriage or female genital mutilation. In such instances, cultural relativism often appears to be a *safer* pathway for development practitioners to maintain local legitimacy and avoid controversy (see Nussbaum, 2011). Current religious partnerships may also function as a form of cultural relativism as development organisations increasingly rely on them as expert judges on internal practices in recipient countries. Development literature in favour of such partnerships has argued that they may offer culturally embedded and thus more appropriate approaches to achieve gender equality. However, all cultures are dynamic and internally diverse. Navigating such complexities requires more than a few select religious partners and culturally relativistic mindset.

Considerations of religion in today's development discourses: The assumption that religion is a purely private matter and will eventually disappear in the course of modernisation continues to infiltrate contemporary development discourses (Tomalin, 2015b). At the same time, Western secular frameworks are themselves rooted in Christian values. The uncritical claim of development organisations to be secular likely obscures their own religious biases (see Clarke et al., 2008). Hadden (1987) argues that development never had a strictly secular departure point. This acknowledgement, he argues, is key to a critical review of the features that are so easily associated with secularism, such as progress and objectivity. Through development interventions, donor countries export their values to developing countries. This has implications for the 'neutrality' that is typically claimed by the development industry.

While seemingly oblivious to their own religious roots, development institutions have been prompted to accept that religion motivates and provides responses to poverty, natural disasters, and human rights violations. At least on paper, a process from estrangement to engagement began (Clarke and Jennings, 2008) spanning Ver Beek's (2000: 31) proclamation that religion was a 'development taboo' to Jones and Petersen's (2011) conclusion that the taboo had been broken a decade later. In 2000, Ver Beek had found that many of the major development studies journals and development organisations consciously chose to avoid the subject of religion. A decade later, Jones and Petersen (2011: 1292) argued that the taboo had been reversed so sharply that it in fact had 'become overly fashionable to talk about religion in development'. Similarly, Tomalin (2011) suggests that there is a sudden hurry amongst development donors to engage with religion after decades of deliberately avoiding it. The first major international initiative marking the recognition of religion in the development process was the World Faith Development Dialogue created in 1998 by the World Bank. It brought together religious leaders and development institution executives to explore potential partnerships (Tomalin, 2015b). Over the next years, international organisations published policy documents on religious partnerships, such as the United Nations Population Fund's 'Guidelines for Engaging Faith-Based Organizations as Cultural Agents of Change' (UNFPA, 2009). Similarly, the UK Foreign, Commonwealth & Development Office (formerly DFID) produced a paper series to guide its work with FBOs, based on 'mutual understanding and respect' (DFID, 2012). Many bilateral development aid organisations also launched interdepartmental centres dedicated to partnerships with faith-based actors and communities, such as the United States Agency for International Development's Center for Faith-Based and Community Initiatives or the German Government initiation of the International Partnership on Religion and Sustainable Development (PaRD).

Development literature also started to engage with the subject as evident from 'the growing number of conferences, seminars, articles, reports and books dealing with religion and development' (Jones and Petersen, 2011: 1292). Swart and Nell (2016: 1) illustrate the 'extraordinary rise of religion and development as a subject field' by providing a chronological bibliography of literature published on this subject since the early to mid-2000s. Development research has engaged in an effort to make religious practices, people, and institutions visible across a range of development-related themes (see, e.g., Manzur et al., 2013 on finance and banking; Nelson, 2011 on education; Bhatewara and Bradley, 2013 on community development). Much of the exiting research has linked religiosity to poverty. For example, in 2000, the World Bank study 'Voices of the Poor' (Narayan et al., 2000) interviewed several thousand people in developing countries around the world to ask them about their experiences of poverty. The interview responses illustrate the centrality of religion in people's lives. Participants repeatedly mentioned 'God', 'prayer', and 'belief' when discussing what gave meaning to their lives (ibid: 25, 188). While the report itself did not specifically discuss this pattern, subsequent development literature has built on such research to highlight the role religion plays in the lives of poor people. For example, Walker (2011: 66) has called on development practitioners to 'understand the significance of religion for many women who live in poverty' (also see Deneulin and Rakodi, 2011: 48). Following in Marx's (1976) footsteps, such research suggests that religion is a refuge for poor people away from the harsh conditions of their daily lives. In so-called 'developed' nations a rise in religiosity is rarely explained by poverty alone. For example, Lewis (2014) and Hirschl et al. (2012) discuss a rise of conservative religious influence in Western politics. Their analysis recognises that there are a series of complex interactions of diverse forces at play. Evidence-based research would unlikely argue that people in the West who vote for politicians who represent religiously conservative values do so simply because they are poor. The same nuance must be applied when attempting to explain the roles that religions play in the lives of people in low-income countries.

There is research that demonstrates a longer-term commitment to making religion's role visible throughout the development process. Parsitau (2011), for example, draws attention to the tendency of local religious leaders to be better positioned to engage in issues that are considered too sensitive or stigmatised to openly share with external actors. As an example, she refers to the case of female internally displaced Kikuyu victims of sexual and gender-based violence, in which only religious communities were able to provide trauma counselling. The Berkely Centre for Religion, Peace, and World Affairs (2010) similarly found that in Bangladesh the promotion of HIV prevention worked best when carried out by local Imams, who have been trained to discuss issues, such as reproductive health, gender empowerment, and HIV. Finally, the recent PaRD-JLI research study which was referenced earlier offers a series of case studies of religious actors facilitating development goals and the barriers they face (Khalaf-Elledge, 2021).

But despite the evidence provided by development research and the recognition among development institutions on paper that the relationship between religion and development needs to be taken seriously (Tomalin, 2015a), integrating religion into development practice has proven to be difficult and little attempted. This could perhaps be explained by the prevailing idea of religion as a *toxic* brand amongst secular-minded development practitioners and policymakers (Woodhead and Catto, 2012). For example, James (2011: 9) argues that '[m]ost governments still view development as a secular enterprise' and 'remain concerned about the spiritual dimensions of faith' in the context of development work. A study of the UK Department of International Development also highlighted the worry of staff about an 'erosion of [the organisation's] traditional secularism' while being dragged into "sectarian and divisive agendas"' (Clarke et al., 2008: 262). Chapter 6 of this book is dedicated entirely to the adverse attitudes of development practitioners towards religion. Additionally – or perhaps consequently – after decades of the negligence of religion, development organisations are 'poorly equipped to deal with religion when they encounter it' (Tomalin, 2015a: 3).

Partnerships with FBOs in development: The extent to which religion is considered in current development processes is virtually limited to the formation of partnerships with faith-based organisations (FBOs). A body of literature has emerged which highlights the different elements of these complex religious organisations (Clarke et al., 2008; Fiddian-Qasmiyeh, 2015; Schnable, 2016). Clarke et al. (2008: 6) define FBOs as 'any organisation that derives inspiration from and guidance for its activities from the teaching and principles of faith or from a particular interpretation or school of thought within a faith'. According to Clark and Jennings (2008), FBOs can take five different functions: faith-based representative organisations, faith-based charitable or development organisations, faith-based sociopolitical organisations, faith-based missionary organisations, and faith-based radical, illegal, or terrorist organisations.[1] Charitable or development FBOs have provided a platform for communities to exercise their religious charity duties; for instance, donations to people in need are now frequently made through FBOs rather than direct giving. With funds received, FBOs undertake a series of activities to assist the poor (Occhipinti, 2015). Clarke (2006: 845) notes that FBOs have a particular advantage compared to secular peers because they can 'draw on elaborate spiritual and moral values' and, due to their well-established networks, can mobilise 'adherents otherwise estranged by secular development discourse'. In the contemporary development arena, many FBOs are keen to move away from merely providing short-term assistance to people in need. FBOs explicitly adopt the language of international development and strive to demonstrate that their work engages people in ways that could enable them to take their own development forward and contribute to long-term sustainable change (Deacon and Tomalin, 2015). Meanwhile, development donors now seem in a 'hurry' to engage with FBOs after decades of consciously ignoring religion (Pearson and Tomalin, 2008: 47).

While discussing FBO partnerships in development, it is important to consider the heteronormativity of FBOs and blurred boundaries between FBOs of different functions. Dinham and Lowndes (2008: 840) flag the tendency of referring to FBOs as a homogenous group and warn that such homogenising 'fails to capture the diversity between, and also importantly within, faiths'. Dinham and Lowndes (2008: 24), therefore, question the idea that all FBOs would act in 'an autonomous and standardized fashion within the public policy arena'. Occhipinti (2015) supports this observation by arguing that the boundaries between the diverse types of FBOs are not always clear; that FBOs can incorporate multiple and overlapping functions; and that FBOs' charitable, missionary, and sociopolitical motivations may conflict. Tadros (2010: 1) points out that especially when it comes to sensitive issues such as gender, FBOs are difficult to classify, since a single organisation can hold multiple diverging standpoints on gender agendas. Furthermore, some organisations may not recognise their own faith-based function, since faith is so integral in the community that they live in and such faith may be indistinguishable from the community's broader social, cultural, and political life. The fluidity within FBOs' organisational identity can make it more difficult for development donors to find and establish partnerships with an FBO that shares similar development goals (Tomalin, 2015a). There is a continuous need to draw attention to the literature that explores how religion is employed outside of traditional religious structures. Schnable (2016) argues that many grassroots NGOs, not only the explicitly faith-based organisations, draw on religious frameworks, networks, and mode of actions to appeal to a broader audience.

Despite increased collaboration, the relationship between FBOs and traditional development donor agencies has been characterised by mutual scepticism. FBOs are known to adhere to religious teachings, while donor policies traditionally claim to be secular or in line with their own religious backgrounds. Government policies have often associated FBO partnerships with a security framework that considers FBOs' actions from a political and ideological rather than humanitarian standpoint (Fiddian-Qasmiyeh, 2015). As a result, the support of FBOs has often been tied to non-economic conditionalities, such as a commitment to secular principles, non-proselytisation, and impartial delivery of aid, which has amplified existing mutual suspicion and scepticism (Fiddian-Qasmiyeh, 2015).

In the absence of trust-based partnerships, the relationship between development and FBOs has remained largely superficial and transactional. Development organisations have shown particular interest in leveraging FBOs' well-established networks, local legitimacy, and outreach channels. Deneulin and Bano (2009) warn that bringing religion and development together has opened up opportunities for negative instrumentalism as well as the danger of development policymakers and practitioners choosing *which* religion they engage with. This choice is more likely to be in line with donors' own values and what is perceived as more familiar and less threatening, rather than with realities on the ground (Clarke et al., 2008). Clarke (2006: 836), for example, voiced concern that development actors tend to liaise with FBOs that are tied to Catholic or liberal Protestant religions more than with other faith traditions. Occhipinti (2015: 333), likewise, noted the failure of Western development actors to recognise their own religious bias towards Christian traditions, as well as their struggle to deal and engage with unfamiliar religious traditions.

The negative gender impacts of development's current religious partnerships

The gender effects of religious partnerships have received particular attention in development literature. Tomalin (2015b) contends:

> it is crucial to view the 'turn to religion' by mainstream development actors through a gendered lens, not only because women are more vulnerable to poverty but because, as some observers have expressed, 'religions have a male' face in many manifestations of the contemporary global religious revival.
>
> (Tomalin, 2011; Tomalin, 2015a: 66)

Scholars have warned that gender implications of FBO partnerships have not been sufficiently considered by practitioners (Tomalin, 2011: 6, 128, also see Tadros, 2010; Occhipinti, 2015). Some fear that a rush to religion without careful research risks that religious partnerships 'exacerbat[e] already fragile gender regimes' (Tomalin, 2011: 134). Occhipinti (2015) writes that the problem lies in the fact that currently FBOs are either dismissed or uncritically supported. Tomalin also warns of the danger of uncritically adopting dominant and typically male perspectives within religious traditions, as this is likely to marginalise other perspectives such as feminist or gender-equal religious interpretations. Both Tomalin (2011: 129) and Tadros (2011: 6) argue that development aid agencies are currently unable to respond to gender bias in religious institutions: the fear of 'openly

criticising religious organisations for their attitudes towards gender' arguably remains one of the biggest perceived problems of secular development
organisations (Tomalin, 2011: 129). Subsequently, feminist development
literature has voiced fear of an early idealisation of FBO's inclusion into
development and instead focused on religion's compatibility with gendered
development goals. Tadros (2010: 1) doubts the ability of FBOs to be 'positive agents for the advancement of gender equality'. She worries about the
patriarchal character of many FBOs leading them to exclude women from
decision-making processes. Tadros argues that in such cases, FBOs share the
blame for women's low levels of agency and power due to their limited participation within FBOs. She also points out that religious actors often refuse
to engage with individuals and social groups who do not comply with norms
regarding gender and sexuality. Seguino (2011: 1317) similarly argues that
'religious non-governmental organisations have a weaker record in improving women's relative well-being than non-religious organisations'.

To the contrary, others have criticised development approaches for
'paint[ing] religious actors with one brush' as conservative, consumed
by tradition, and resisting change (Ferris, 2011: 623). Similarly, Fiddian-
Qasmiyeh (2015: 569) argues that beneficiaries' religious beliefs and practices have been rejected on the assumption that they are so deeply embedded in 'their patriarchal oppressive structures that "they" are suffering from
false consciousness that only "we" can overcome'. She calls for more evidence to prove that FBOs are automatically more conservative and more
likely to endorse gender inequality. Fiddian-Qasmiyeh (2015: 563) points
to the history of repression of secular organisations and argues that secular
programmes may be just as gender biased. Clayton and Stanton's (2008:
114) assertion that secularism is misconceived as 'objective' and 'natural'
supports this argument. Their work suggests that secularism makes assumptions about 'God, the world and humanity just like any other worldview'
and that 'the absence of God does not make it objective, nor does the pres-
ence of God in other worldviews make them more subjective'. Day and
Coleman (2013) equally assert that the 'secular', just like religion, is 'culturally constructed category, ideology, and even set of practices'.

Overall, arguments have been made both for and against the inclusion
of religious actors into gender-related development work. This debate is
problematic because it again lumps FBOs together despite their – at times –
immense differences. Secular organisations can equally sustain systems
that impede gender equality. Additionally, the religious and secular realm
is often impossible to distinguish. Regardless of the outcome of this debate,
development scholars agree that religion plays a significant role in societies,
especially when it comes to gender issues. This global phenomenon can no
longer be ignored. The discussion now needs to shift to understanding the

context-specific dynamics of this interaction and how it impacts development issues and donor policies. As part of the collective effort it will take to achieve development's gender goals, *all* partners – whether religious or not – should be selected based on their track record on gender equality issues. Ideally, they have a history of supporting women's rights and tackling gender discrimination (Tomalin, 2007; Tadros, 2010; Bradley, 2011). Development organisations that are themselves permeated by conservative gender ideologies may struggle to successfully implement gender equality goals abroad.

Conclusion

This chapter reviews the role religion plays in development thinking and processes. It considers four dimensions of this relationship: 1. the historic roles of religions in providing social services; 2. religious actors' contributions and hindrance of gendered development goals; 3. the roles that religions have played in Western colonial missions, the post-war secular era, and today's so-called turn to religion; and 4. the negative gendered implications of current religious partnerships. The discussion highlights that religion is not only a recent subject of consideration in the field of development but has historically influenced development aid policies themselves. Currently, the association of religion and poverty remains strong within development discourses, obscuring practitioners' own religious biases. Scholars agree that there is a need for more research on effectively choosing and engaging with religion and FBOs in international development. This is especially needed to curb the gender-regressive effects some of the current partnerships may have.

Note

1   While Clarke et al.'s (2008) typology includes a category for *radical, illegal, or terrorist organisations*, some choose to exclude this category as it is not based on organisational but on ideological characteristics and, as such, could potentially cut across all other categories (Le Moigne and Petersen, 2016: 13).

Bibliography

Abu-Lughod, L. (2013). *Do Muslim Women Need Saving?* Cambridge, MA: Harvard University Press.
Bell, L. S, Nathan, A. J., and Peleg, I. (2001). Who Produces Asian Identity? Discourse, Discrimination, and Chinese Peasant Women in the Quest for Human

Rights. In *Negotiating Culture and Human Rights: Beyond Universalism and Relativism*. New York: Columbia University Press.

Berkley Center for Religion, Peace and World Affairs. (2010). *Faith-Inspired Organizations and Global Development Policy: A Background Review "Mapping" Social and Economic Development Work in Europe and Africa*. Available from: http://berkleycenter.georgetown.edu/publications/faith-inspired-organizations-and-global-development-policy-a-background-review-mapping-social-and-economic-development-work-in-europe-and-africa [accessed 14 March 2016].

Bhatewara, Z., and Bradley, T. (2013). The People Know They Need Religion in Order to Develop: Religion's Capacity to Inspire People in Pune's Slums. *European Journal of Development Research*, 25(2): 288–304.

Boas, F. (1887). Museums of Ethnology and Their Classification. *Science*, 9: 589.

Bradley, T. (2011). *Religion and Gender in the Developing World: Faith-Based Organizations and Feminism in India*. London: I.B. Tauris.

Clarke, G. (2006). Faith Matters: Faith-Based Organizations, Civil Society and International Development. *Journal of International Development*, 18(6): 835–848.

Clarke, G., and Jennings, M. (eds.). (2008). *Development, Civil Society and Faith-based Organizations. Bridging the Sacred and the Secular*. Basingstoke: Palgrave Macmillan.

Clarke, G., Jennings, M., and Shaw, T. (2008). *Development, Civil Society and Faith-Based Organizations: Bridging the Sacred and the Secular*. London: Palgrave Macmillan.

Clayton, M., and Stanton, N. (2008). The Changing World's View of Christian Youth Work. *Youth and Policy*, 100: 109–118.

Day, A., and Coleman, S. (2013). Secularization. In *Oxford Bibliographies Online: Anthropology*. New York: Oxford University Press.

Deacon, G., and Tomalin, E. (2015). A History of Faith-Based Aid and Development. In E. Tomalin (ed.), *The Routledge Handbook on Religions and Global Development*. London and New York: Routledge.

Deneulin, S., and Bano, M. (2009). *Religion in Development: Rewriting the Secular Script*. London: Zed Books.

Deneulin, S., and Rakodi, C. (2011). Revisiting Religion: Development Studies Thirty Years on. *World Development*, 39(1): 45–54.

DFID. (2012). *Faith Partnership Principles: Working Effectively with Faith Groups to Fight Global Poverty*. London: Department for International Development.

Dinham, A., and Lowndes, V. (2008). Religion, Resources and Representation: Three Narratives of Engagement in British Urban Governance. *Urban Affairs Review*, 43(6): 817–845.

Ferris, E. (2005). *Faith-Based and Secular Humanitarian Organizations, International Review of the Red Cross*. Available from: www.icrc.org/eng/resources/documents/article/review/review-858-p311.htm [accessed 3 April 2018].

Ferris, E. (2011). Faith and Humanitarianism: It's Complicated. *Journal of Refugee Studies*, 24(3): 606–625.

Fiddian-Qasmiyeh, E. (2015). Engendering Understandings of Faith-Based Organisations: Intersections Between Religion and Gender in Development and

64 *Why the religion–gender nexus matters*

Humanitarian Interventions. In A. Coles, L. Gray, and J. Momsen (eds.), *Routledge Handbook of Gender and Development*. London: Routledge.

Goulet, D. (1980). Development Experts: The One-Eyed Giants. *World Development*, 8(7–8): 481–489.

Hadden, J. K. (1987). Toward Desacralizing Secularization Theory. *Social Forces*, 65(3): 587–611.

Hirschl, T. A., Booth, J. G., Glenna, L. L., and Green, B. Q. (2012). Politics, Religion, and Society: Is the United States Experiencing a Period of Religious-Politi cal Polarization? *Review of European Studies*, 4(4): 95–109.

James, R. (2011). Handle with Care: Engaging with Faith-Based Organisations in Development. *Development in Practice*, 21(1): 109–117.

Jones, B., and Petersen, M. J. (2011). Instrumental, Narrow, Normative? Reviewing Recent Work on Religion and Development. *Third World Quarterly*, 32(7): 1291–1306.

Khalaf-Elledge, N. (2021). *Scoping Study: Looking Back to Look Forward. The Role of Religious Actors in Gender Equality since the Beijing Declaration*. Washington, DC: Joint Learning Initiative on Faith and Local Communities (JLI).

Lewis, A. R. (2014). Abortion Politics and the Decline of the Separation of Church and State: The Southern Baptist Case. *Politics and Religion*, 7: 521–549.

Manzur, D., Meisami, H., and Roayaee, M. (2013). Banking for the Poor in the Context of Islamic Finance. *Journal of Contemporary Management*, 2(2): 53–70.

Marx, K. [1844] (1976). Introduction to A Contribution to the Critique of Hegel's Philosophy of Right. In *Collected Works*, vol. 3. New York: International Publishers.

McKay, J. (2004). Reassessing Development Theory: 'Modernisation' and Beyond. In D. J. Kingsbury, J. Remenyi, J. McKay, and J. Hunt (eds.), *Key Issues in Development*. Basingstoke: Palgrave Macmillan.

Narayan, D., Chambers, R., Shah, M. K., and Petesch, P. (2000). *Voices of the Poor: Crying Out for Change*. New York: Oxford University Press.

Nelson, M. J. (2011). Secularism and the Sacred: Partners in Education-for-Development. *Comparative Education Review*, 55(1): 129–131.

Nussbaum, M. C. (2011). *Creating Capabilities: The Human Development Approach*. Cambridge, MA: The Belknap Press of Harvard University Press.

Occhipinti, L. A. (2015). Faith-Based Organisations and Development. In E. Tomalin (ed.), *The Routledge Handbook on Religions and Global Development*. London and New York: Routledge.

Parsitau, D. (2011). The Role of Faith and Faith-Based Organisations Among Internally Displaced Persons in Kenya. *Journal of Refugee Studies*, 24(3): 473–492.

Pearson, R., and Tomalin, E. (2008). Intelligent Design? A Gender-Sensitive Interrogation of Religion and *Development*. In G. Clarke and M. Jennings (eds.), *Development, Civil Society and Faith-Based Organizations: Bridging the Sacred and the Secular*. London: Palgrave Macmillan.

Reid-Henry, S. (2012). Neoliberalism's 'Trade Not Aid' Approach to Development Ignored Past Lessons. *The Guardian*, 30 October. Available from: www.theguardian.com/global-development/2012/oct/30/neoliberalism-approach-development-ignored-past-lessons [accessed 26 September 2013].

Religion in development and its gender impact   65

Said, E. (2003). *Preface to the Twenty-Fifth Anniversary Edition. Orientalism.* New York: Penguin.

Schnable, A. (2016). Frames, Modes of Action, Networks: What Religion Affords Grassroots NGOs. *Journal for the Scientific Study of Religion*, 55(2): 216–232.

Seguino, S. (2011). Help or Hindrance? Religion's Impact on Gender Inequality. *World Development*, 39(8): 1308–1321.

Sen, A. (1985). *Commodities and Capabilities.* New Delhi: Oxford University Press.

Sen, A. (2006). *Identity and Violence.* New York: W. W. Norton.

Spivak, G. C. (1993). *Can the Subaltern Speak?* In P. Williams and L. Chrisman (eds.), *Colonial Discourse and Postcolonial Theory.* New York: Harvester Wheatsheaf.

Swart, I., and Nell, E. (2016). Religion and Development: The Rise of a Bibliography. *HTS Teologiese Studies/Theological Studies* [S.l.] 72: 4.

Tadros, M. (2010). *Faith-Based Organisations and Service Delivery: Some Gender Conundrums.* Geneva: UNRISD.

Tadros, M. (2011). Religion, Rights and Gender at the Crossroads. *IDS Bulletin*, 42(1).

Tomalin, E. (2007). *Gender Studies Approaches to the Relationships Between Religion and Development.* RaD Working Papers Series 4. Birmingham: University of Birmingham.

Tomalin, E. (2011). *Gender, Faith and Development.* Oxford: Oxfam.

Tomalin, E. (ed.). (2015a). *The Routledge Handbook on Religions and Global Development.* London and New York: Routledge.

Tomalin, E. (2015b). Gender, Development and the 'De-Privatization' of Religion'. In R. Bush, P. Fountain, and M. Feener (eds.), *Religion and the Politics of Development: Priests, Potentates, and 'Progress'.* Palgrave Macmillan.

UNFPA. (2009). *Guidelines for Engaging FBOs as Agents of Change.* Available from: www.unfpa.org/sites/default/files/resource-pdf/fbo_engagement.pdf [accessed 21 February 2018].

Ver Beek, K. A. (2000). Spirituality: A Development Taboo. *Development in Practice*, 10(1): 31–43.

Volpp, L. (2001). Feminism Versus Multiculturalism. *Columbia Law Review*, 101(5): 1181–1218.

Walker, B. (2011). Christianity, Development, and Women's Liberation'. In E. Tomalin (ed.), *Gender, Faith and Development.* Rugby, UK: Practical Action Publishing.

Woodhead, L., and Catto, R. (eds.). (2012). *Religion and Change in Modern Britain.* London: Routledge.

Part II

How to engage with the religion–gender nexus in development policy and practice

4 Realising religious literacy

Moving beyond religious partnerships

Development literature has praised the 'emerging openness to thinking about and engaging with religion in development' (Tomalin, 2011: 134). For example, Bradley (2011) writes that issues related to religion are increasingly considered including in the context of gender. Deneulin and Rakodi (2011: 52) argue that 'in some ways, development studies is well equipped to understand the complex and context-dependent ways in which religion influences people's lives'.

My research finds that while development theory may be somewhat equipped to consider religion's diverse influences in society, development practitioners are far from being adequately prepared. Currently, there is less of an openness to thinking about *religion* than an openness to engaging in *partnerships*, which had always been an integral part of development. Engagement with religion outside of partnerships was negligible and, by research participants' own accounts, based on simplifications, generalisations, and presumptions. That was particularly noticeable when organisations select religious partners. Partner selection did not follow a standard procedure and covered only a small fraction of the religious landscape. This means that through partnering with FBOs or religious leaders, development organisations not only are outsourcing the responsibility to acquire knowledge on religion but the narrow selection of partners also skews the outcomes of this knowledge building. Current religious partnerships create a false illusion of religious homogeneity and perpetuate misconceptions about internally diverse religions that are deeply embedded in all dimensions of society. Additionally, rushed and uninformed selections of partners have had adverse gender effects.

In this chapter, I discuss the need for improved and self-reflective religious literacy prior to religious partnerships. I use the term religious literacy in conjunction with the term self-reflection to highlight that religious literacy in development needs to move beyond mere knowledge building.

DOI: 10.4324/9781003112549-5

Religious literacy must include a critical analysis and acknowledgement of one's own viewpoints and biases and how these may affect one's understandings of religions. This chapter draws on Moore's and Dinham's theoretical frameworks and provides a guide for development organisations and practitioners to build self-reflective religious literacy and be ready to address complex religious dynamics when they encounter them.

Why does development need self-reflective religious literacy?

Development organisations interviewed for this research did not have official guidelines for partner selection in place. Most participants described the in-country selection of their partners as a case-to-case scenario mostly depending on 'who is the most obvious?', 'who do we already know?', and 'who does the donor like?'. Partners were selected before the start of a project, well before actual religious contexts could be understood. Such rushed partner selection is arguably pushed by the global policy to 'turn to religion' which proclaims that religious actors are an integral part of development assistance and, as such, should be included in all development intervention. As such, the selection of religious partners functions similarly to gender checklists in development. This pre-emptive approach does not allow for a comprehensive analysis and context-based understanding of religion. Its pre-emptive nature may do more harm than good and highlights a bigger emphasis on partnerships than religious literacy. Only one government aid agency could offer an example of a research-based selection process of religious partners. The participant of this agency, Ellen, argued that religious partners form an important part of development work; however, sometimes the need for them is clearer than at other times. She gave the example of working on the Family Law in Zanzibar, which includes both Custom and Religious and Statutory Law. After studying the context, the government aid agency decided to partner with specific religious leaders and women's rights lawyers. 'These were obviously the partners you needed to work with' Ellen explained.

Disregarding the dynamic roles that religions play in society can have serious effects, especially for gender goals in development. Religion, through the way it is interpreted and appropriated by some, can mask and legitimise gender inequality. At the same time, religions have also been interpreted in support of gender equality. Development practitioners have to be aware of such competing claims, especially since they are typically not equally visible. Religiously powerful voices within a community are often male and do not automatically reflect the most gender-progressive or gender-equal interpretations of their religion. Currently, development practitioners have difficulties comprehending and navigating conflicting truth claims. Instead, practitioners often treat what they encounter in the field as universal truths which in turn triggers confusion and misconceptions. It can lead to a partner selection that further marginalises feminist voices. A lack of religious literacy may also lead development practitioners to disproportionately call religion out by name in negative, gender-regressive, or conflict scenarios. As a result, practitioners could – accidentally – obscure the dynamic and diverse nature of religions. When religious influences are progressive, they are often described as 'Western-style feminist' or in line with 'Western progressive values'. This confirmation bias renders the role religions play in 'positive' situations unrecognised and thus invisible (Khalaf-Elledge, 2020). Some journal articles still classify women in Muslim countries as either 'Westernised elite' or 'Muslim women' based on how liberal they are. This overlooks the possibility of Muslim women to be both liberal and feminist without being Westernised. In other words, one does not cease to be Muslim when one exhibits similar traits to those claimed as Western. Self-reflective religious literacy helps expand development's understanding of what it means to be Muslim, which reflects a wide and nuanced spectrum just like any other religious identity. Self-reflective religious literacy can enable practitioners to make sense of the seemingly contradictory ways in which religion interacts with other social issues, such as gender. It allows for a better understanding of the complex contexts that religions exist in, and thus, for more an evidence-based programme approach and partner selection.

Self-reflective religious literacy for development practice

When a growing number of religion scholars identified a lack of religious understanding across fields, such as education, public services, peacebuilding, and community development they started a new discourse to improve current levels of religious literacy (see Prothero, 2007; Moore, 2007; Dinham, 2017; Wright, 1993). Dinham and Francis' (2015) work offers a detailed and useful account of current debates about religious literacy and the need for such a discourse in the first place. They contend that the term 'religious literacy' can contain a wide range of meanings and is thus used rather vaguely. Religious literacy is a relatively young discourse and has been applied differently by different people. For example, Prothero focuses on knowledge of the basic tenants of religion and argues that the wider American public needs to be better informed on religion to foster democratic processes in the country. Moore (2007) broadens this scope and centres her attention on the ability to understand diverse manifestations of religion in contemporary sociopolitics with the aim of peacebuilding. A core feature of her framework is the recognition that religious ideas and practices are context dependent and historically situated. Or as Conroy (2015: 169) suggests, religious literacy means 'the capacity to locate particular ideas within their historical, ethical, epistemological and social context'. Dinham's (2017) conceptualisation of religious literacy similarly goes beyond a call for mere knowledge building. It focuses on improving the conversation between religious and non-religious actors and entails a change in personal attitudes. The challenge that remains is for this discourse to be both 'thoughtful and theorised' while still 'publicly accessible and practical' (Dinham, 2017: 258). There is a pressing need to bridge the gap between theoretical frameworks of religious literacy and mainstream public understanding of religion (Moore, 2017).

The idea of religious literacy has not yet been introduced into development theory but, as outlined earlier, appears essential to its practice. Development organisations that train their mainstream staff in religious literacy are currently a trivial exception and self-reflection is virtually never an element of such training. In the following, I list seven key principles of self-reflective religious literacy that are indispensable for development practitioners in the context of gender.

1   First and foremost, critical self-reflection is key to building religious literacy. This entails understanding 'one's assumptions and how they may affect a conversation on and a personal relation to religion' (Dinham and Francis, 2015: 267). For example, if one's own predisposition is that secularism is neutral and is the norm, then one is likely to perceive religion as subjective and external. I discuss practitioners' personal biases towards religion in detail in Chapter 6. As an industry, development disproportionately frames religion within a security framework. Dinham and Francis (2015: 7) observe a current 'anxiety about extremism [which] casts religion and belief as a problem'. According to participants in my research, development also has largely focused on religion in the contexts of security, peacebuilding, or cohesion agendas. The contexts in which religion is addressed frames the nature of the discussion around it. Of course, religious partnerships are also considered in other areas, such as gender-based violence, family planning, or child marriage, but there too, religious partnerships are formed mainly because religion is perceived to be the problem. Tomalin flags the 'religion as obstacle' approach throughout development discourses and criticises a 'proliferation of interest' in issues around security, fundamentalism, and human rights when talking about religion (Tomalin, 2007: 26).

2   Religious literacy is not the same as 'being religious'. Both Dinham (2016) and Moore (2015) lament that all too often an academic study of religion is confused with devotional expressions of it. This distinction is important as it acknowledges the 'validity of normative theological assertions without equating them with universal truths about the tradition itself' (Moore, 2015: 7). For example, a devotional expression would be to say 'God sent his only son, Jesus, to save us'. An academic study would say 'the belief that Jesus is God's son is foundational in the Christian belief system'. Moore (2015: 37) is not saying that religious people are less able to study religions academically, but she criticises the automatic assumption that 'practitioners of a given religious tradition are . . . the best sources of information about the tradition' as well as the tendency to consider them 'formally or informally as "experts"'. Dinham (2016) similarly advises that '[w]e should not assume that being religious gives people religious literacy'. My research findings indicate that this assumption, nonetheless, continues to be widespread in development. For example, after a gender discussion with leaders from the Catholic Church, Patrick, a government aid agency participant said:

> I think that's one of the pluses of being able to work with faith groups [to] have a real better understanding of social norms and traditional practices of the religion.

However, the understanding that was acquired here refers to a Christian worldview, more specifically, a small fraction of Catholic organised religion in the West. This narrow sample of a particular religious worldview cannot replace an academic study of religion. In this sense, one could argue that the way some religious partnerships are currently used in development constitutes a devotional rather than a non-sectarian and academic study.

While religious individuals are not automatically more religiously literate, neither are those who embrace other specific worldviews like secularism, atheism, or agnosticism. Because of the many different viewpoints that exist when it comes to religion, the discourse on religious literacy has been accompanied by the question of 'who should be doing it?'. Dinham deliberates:

> A tempting answer for many in the West has been that it is best done in some kind of secular way which reflects a wider idea that secularity somehow equals neutrality, and that this is an essential condition for the impartial inclusion of all. But nobody starts from nowhere and there is no such thing as neutrality.
>
> (Dinham, 2017: 259)

The assumption that secularism offers a neutral framework of analysis is widespread. Moore argues that this misconception stems from the Enlightenment period and the definitions of secularism that became influential in the aftermath of colonialism and still remain deeply embedded in today's public discourses around the globe (Moore, 2015: 37). Assuming that secularism is a neutral starting point obstructs a truthful engagement with religion. Consequently, Dinham (2017: 259) recommend that religious literacy must also entail an exploration of 'assumed secularity':

> The secular is a normative notion, and is as much misunderstood as religion itself. Secular literacy is an inescapable part of religious literacy because secularity is the assumed context of religiousness. Religious literacy requires clarity about what both concepts could mean.

The answer to 'who should be doing religious literacy' in the context of development would be 'everyone'. It is not so much about 'knowing everything', as about 'having the confidence and wherewithal to know who and what to ask' (Dinham, 2017: 212) as well as the recognition that there is no neutral departure point.

3   Religions are internally diverse. Beliefs and practices differ widely between and also *within* religions. Generalising about and homogenising entire religions fails to capture this diversity (Dinham and Lowndes, 2008: 8, 24). A literature review of academic literature and development reporting indicates that Western development discourses generally acknowledge differences within the Christian faith much better, but tend to homogenise when it comes to other religions. For example, donor documents frequently refer to the 'Muslim World' as if it were a distant, isolated, and homogenous entity (Khalaf-Elledge, 2020).

The overwhelming majority of local activists in my sample were well aware of religions' internal diversity. For example, a women's rights activist from my research sample deliberated:

> If you actually speak to people and listen to different groups there will be loads of different voices, but there's an assumption that everybody in the community thinks the same and worships the same.

She explained that 'it takes a bit more work to map out the actual situation' than what is currently done by development organisations. Much of the religious diversity and nuance remains unexplored in donor-funded activities while the focus continues to be on forming partnership rather than religious literacy. The document analysis of my research indicates similar patterns: when discussing the role of religious partnerships for development, many government aid agencies used the term 'Christian' almost interchangeably with 'religious', without explicitly acknowledging such bias. For example, many donor reports repeatedly referred to large Christian organisations when explaining the unique societal roles of FBOs. One report referred to the World Council of Churches (WCC) when outlining its 2030 agenda and rationale for global religious partnerships. It subsequently argued that religious organisations and partners can do the following:

- promote the inclusion of different groups;
- offer peaceful channels for conflict resolution;
- uphold the human rights of the most vulnerable;
- remind political leaders of their duty to enable all people to realise their rights;
- help ensure that investment takes place in communities;
- mobilise people everywhere, especially young people;
- share expertise on how to deliver services to those who are hardest to reach.

Solely referencing the WCC not only demonstrates the government agency's proximity to the Christian faith but also implies the assumption of homogenous behaviour of all FBOs.

At this point, it is worth acknowledging the shortcomings of the term FBO itself. As discussed in the previous chapter, the term implies that FBOs form a homogenous group and act the same way everywhere. But just like other non-governmental organisations, FBOs can differ greatly from one another. Moreover, the label 'faith', which is frequently used in donor reporting, has Christian roots. The term has little relevance 'outside Western Christian contexts' (Hefferan, 2015: 41). Likewise, Jeavons (2004: 141) argues that, in other religions, 'faith is not a particularly meaningful concept or term'.

The overwhelming majority of religious partners of organisations in my sample were Christian affiliated and based out of Western countries. Notably, almost all of the contracts of the six government aid agencies in my sample were concentrated in two Western Christian international FBOs. Clarke identified similar trends in a study in 2007. He noted that almost the entire FBO funding of one European government donor was given to only two Christian international FBOs, 'even where the local community was not Christian' (Clarke, 2007: 87). The landscape of religious partnerships has not changed much since Clarke's study and still exhibits the same big players. Many government aid agencies in my sample routinely used the same religious partners on long-term retainers, both at the international and local levels. Some of these partnerships were more than a decade old. When asked about this imbalance, research participants said that their networks of Christian organisations date much further back and are well established. They are only now beginning to branch out into other religions. Some participants also explained that they considered Christian partners to be more familiar with Western ideas of development. They felt it was easier to identify them and form lasting partnerships with them. The result is that religious partners in development today only represent select voices of the wide and diverse religious landscape prevalent in recipient countries. Nevertheless, they are labelled 'faith partnerships' (rather than Christian-Western partnerships) and, as such, are sufficient to tick-the-box of development organisations' calls to integrate religion into their work.

4   Religions have blurred boundaries. They are all-encompassing and cannot be meaningfully separated from the secular realm or from the cultural, social, or political views of their followers. As one of the participants put it:

> religion doesn't exist outside of people . . . it's how people practice it, how people talk about it, how people live it.
>
> (Marlene, Women's rights activist, UK)

McGuire (2008), among others, challenges the constructed boundaries scholars infer when defining religion and warns of the danger of 'adopting an overly institutional – and historically inaccurate – view of religion'. Such perspectives assume that religion is a defined entity with distinguishable features. Instead, McGuire demonstrates the 'messy' and – often – contradictory realities of religious practices and experiences in people's everyday lives. Therefore, scholars recommend that religion should be considered as a *lived* concept with no set boundaries (McGuire, 2008; Sharafeldin, 2013; Bishop, 2016). Schnable (2016) also explores religion beyond traditional structures and argues that a whole range of grassroots organisations – not only FBOs – use religious frameworks, networks, and modes of actions. Many organisations navigate between both secular and religious realms every day. Schnable draws on local practices and experience to highlight the varied and cross-cutting areas in which religion and 'secular' development overlap. Tomalin (2012: 694) points to the Christian origins of this idea:

The very act of distinguishing between 'faith-based' and secular organizations in contexts where religion may permeate almost all aspects of life is arguably an imposition of Christianised or Western understandings of the relationship between the religious and the secular that do not have the same meaning elsewhere.

5   All religious interpretations are subject to change and are deeply embedded in and intertwined with political, historical, and socioeconomic contexts (Moore, 2015). This means that 'the same religions and beliefs are different in different people and places' (Dinham et al., 2017: 3). This element of religious literacy is especially relevant when studying the intersection of religion and gender. It explains why religions are internally so diverse. All religions have changed throughout history and have been adapted to how humans live their lives, what values they hold, and how they structure their societies. Interpretations of the same religion differ particularly in the context of gender issues, which in turn are central to how a society is run. For example, Christians have different views when it comes to contraception, samesex marriage, or women pastors. There is not one single interpretation of the Bible on these issues that every Christian subscribes to. How Christians interpret these issues may depend on their personal belief systems, their upbringing, their political views, or their socio-economic circumstances. Development practitioners navigate different contexts and encounter diverse and often-conflicting interpretations of the same religion. Practitioners will not be able to interview every single member of a social group to understand the entire spectrum of their beliefs. Nevertheless, development practice often makes assumptions about the general tendencies of a group. Maybe this general sense is constructed through conversations with a handful of group members, but more likely practitioners' ideas about a religion stem from previously formed and long-held preconception. This is how development practitioners arrive at a single story of a religion, for example, 'Buddhism is a non-violent religion', 'Muslim women are oppressed', 'Hindus are polythetic', or 'Christianity is more gender equal than other religions'. The biggest danger of homogenising and stereotyping an entire religion is that internal power struggles within that religion may be overlooked and opportunities to support marginalised feminist voices could be forgone. Since religion is currently not part of development's programme repertoire, practitioners' ideas about religion are unlikely based on rigorous evidence-based research. As part of respecting the diversity and dignity of all people, development practitioners urgently need to

recognise the abundance of circumstances that shape the way religion is lived and experienced.

6 Once development practitioners have familiarised themselves with the context-specific expressions of a particular religious group, the next step is to understand the power dynamics enabling and preserving these dynamics. Religion is ubiquitously entangled with power. This entanglement alone is an urgent reason for development to engage with religion, since – at least in theory – development is ultimately about shifting and transforming power balances.

Moore's (2015: 5) framework of religious literacy calls for an analysis of power and powerlessness, asking 'which perspectives are politically and socially prominent and why?', 'which are marginalized or silenced and why?', and 'why is it that some theological interpretations are more accepted than others in relationship to specific issues in particular social/historical contexts?'. Moore (2015: 5) points out that all religious knowledge claims are socially constructed and represent particular situated perspectives. Religious knowledge production is an ongoing and often internally contested process. Understanding who is in charge of producing this knowledge can reveal the larger power structures within a community. Typically, the most powerful voices within a social group assume charge of religious knowledge production and decide which religious interpretations are adequate. A power analysis could show that practices labelled 'religious' may not actually derive from eternal and divine laws but instead serve as social mechanisms to preserve prevalent power structures. Moore uses the example of the Taliban's rise to power in Afghanistan. She highlights that the Taliban's religious claims differ vastly from others within the same religious tradition. Moore encourages reflection on why their gender ideology gained social legitimacy over other competing claims within the country and concludes that power plays a vital role in lending 'credibility and influence to some religious traditions over others' (Moore, 2015: 6).

Following Moore's framework, partnering with organisations inevitably means selecting and empowering specific worldviews over others. By choosing and building partnerships with specific groups, development organisations do weigh in on debates about which knowledge counts, at least for their programme purposes. When it comes to choosing religious organisations, donor funding influences local debates and power struggles over religious interpretations by elevating some voices over others. Development organisations have been criticised for *choosing* which religion they engage with (Clarke et al., 2008). For example, US evangelical non-governmental organisations (NGOs) have been promoting conservative religious interpretations in Uganda suiting the NGOs' own religious agendas while emboldening Uganda's recent regressive anti-gay legislation (Arinaitwe, 2014). There is an urgent need to understand the power structures underpinning the religion-gender nexus, including how religions are used to legitimise systems and laws that undermine equality.

Paradoxically, religious partnerships were often described by participants in research as a *safe* way to incorporate religion without intruding in it. It is uncertain to what extent donors are aware of the existing power dynamics and knowledge production processes within a community, as well as their own interference in them. Based on my findings, building this awareness is not the current focus of development practice. If anything, organisations are preoccupied with diversifying their partner portfolios (e.g., adding non-Christian groups) in an effort to respond to the global policy call to 'turn to religion'. Contracts and partnerships have often emboldened the most powerful and well-connected groups in a country. Most of the women's rights activists in my sample were not at all surprised by this. They are aware of local power dynamics within their communities. Nabila, a Malawian women's rights activist who currently works as a gender consultant for a European government-funded programme, explained that it makes sense for development organisations to work with those in power as they provide the 'best and most influential networks'. Marlene, a women's rights activist in the UK similarly rationalised this approach:

> If it's a country where the government is intertwined with religious bodies or some countries where there's not a clear separation between religion and state then you are always going to have those groups putting themselves in a prominent position to take up work. There might be lots of groups, feminist groups, or very progressive community groups, but they're not going to be the first people that are looked at to work with probably.

7   Religion is often linked to gender issues when it surfaces in the public realm. It is important to note that, throughout history, religions have inspired both patriarchal and emancipatory social changes. So far, religious literacy discourses have paid little attention to gender considerations. This is surprising since the links between gender and religion are well documented in academic literature and many negative assumptions religious literacy seeks to challenge are in fact gender related. For example, religious literacy discourses repeatedly criticise simplified portrayals of religious women but do not include an accompanying

analysis of feminist theories and conceptual links between gender and religion. Nevertheless, since religious literacy is a young discourse, it could well be the case that intersectional issues such as gender or race will be addressed as it continues to grow.

A gender-focused approach to religious literacy is crucial for development. My research identifies multiple examples of situations where a lack of religious literacy during the selection of partners may have caused negative gender effects later on. For example, a research participant recalled a domestic violence project in Jordan funded by a large European government donor. The project employed a range of stakeholders, including a large religious group, and sought to support survivors of domestic violence by setting up women's shelters. Shortly after inception, the leadership of the project was transferred to the religious partner who in turn started to impose conditions on women accessing the shelter. These conditions paradoxically excluded women who were survivors of sexual violence, deeming them unclean. Consequently, women's rights activists involved in the project flagged this to the government donor, whose unresponsiveness led the activists to disengage from the project. This is an example in which the push to select religious partners was not only poorly executed but also took priority over the purpose of the project, which was to support – not stigmatise – women. My research cannot confirm whether this situation occurred solely because of a lack of self-reflective religious literacy, or perhaps also because of perceived political inability to partner with more progressive actors. Nevertheless, my findings show an abundance of such cases. In a different example, a Malawian woman who had reported her husband to the police was told by a project's pastor that she should forgive her husband and ask for him to be released out of custody. Malawi had passed a *Prevention of Domestic Violence* Act in 2006 and has growing feminist movements; yet despite all this, the development project in question chose to partner with a pastor that did not consider domestic violence a serious crime or women's safety and well-being a priority. The Malawian participant, Nabila, conceded that it is indeed difficult to avoid such partners, as they are extremely powerful and are often the sole service providers to communities. Another women's rights activist, Gabriella recalled a similar instance in which the government aid agency she worked with partnered with a priest whose homophobic views led him to exclude LGBTI people from the project. Gabriella remembered feeling helpless as she watched people being discriminated against but found herself unable to take any actions against this. She was instructed by the project leader not to intervene under any circumstances: 'if we don't have this priest's support', the project leader argued 'we lose a lot of respect within the context'. This again signals that partners were selected to appease local power structures and thus gain legitimacy, rather than through informed and self-reflective religious literacy and gender considerations.

Given my research findings, it is fair to assume that the most powerful religious voices in a country do not automatically reflect the most gender-just and politically progressive agendas. The preceding examples illustrate the effect powerful religious partners can have on gender dynamics. While currently not a priority within the religious literacy discourse, there is a growing body of development literature concerned with the gendered implications of religious partnerships (see Chapter 3).

When it comes to gender and religious literacy, Tomalin's (2007, 2011) work could provide valuable suggestions. She reviews literature across academic disciplines that engages with the religious dimension of GAD themes, such as reproductive health, FGM, and HIV/AIDS. Tomalin finds that this literature currently informs neither development theory nor practice. She suggests that development practitioners should have a thorough understanding of the different and competing religious beliefs that influence or do not influence specific gendered practices. They should also pay attention to those religious positions that could be 'compatible with a development agenda that is concerned with poverty reduction and the pursuit of human right' (Tomalin, 2007: 28) and to form partnerships with religious organisations that already advocate for gender equality (also see Bradley, 2011; Tadros, 2010). In 2017, the Association for Women's Rights in Development (AWID) also called on international development to support and partner with those local actors who enable people to 'discuss religious discourses that are congruent with human rights and gender justice' (Imam et al., 2017: 23 on behalf of AWID). While these are useful suggestions, they again require a certain feminist predisposition of development organisations, which cannot be confirmed in my research findings. At the time being, religious partners are not accepted or rejected because of their track record on gender. Development's own commitment to gender currently does not seem strong enough to conduct such a gender vetting of religious partners in the first place. Religious partners are selected primarily because of the instrumental benefits they bring to development efforts. The interviewed women's rights activists also challenged the notion that Western development efforts are automatically progressive and feminist. One of them was Nabila, the women's rights activist from Malawi. She wondered why donors should have the 'political will or desire to engage with very progressive actors anyway' since they 'probably aren't feminists in their own countries'. Nabila shook her head: 'if they're not listening to feminists at home why were they going to be seeking them out in other countries?'

Conclusion

The discussion in this chapter explores key principles of self-reflective religious literacy relevant to gender and development. So far, religious literacy has been largely outsourced to religious partners. However, this can sidetrack internal skill-building, promote select religious voices, and ignore religions' fluid roles outside traditional structures. Given the current rush to religious partners, there is an immediate need for a research agenda concerned with more careful and informed partner selection. In the long term, however, development practitioners must expand their skill set beyond partnership politics and build their own self-reflective religious literacy. It is pivotal that development discourses and practitioners acknowledge and assume responsibility for their active part in shaping religious dynamics and knowledge production.

Development's preference for external religious partners over internal religious literacy building is fostered by the fact that religion continues to be viewed as a unique feature of so-called developing countries. Only when development acknowledges that religion influences social systems worldwide will religion be considered a mainstream issue in development.

Bibliography

Arinaitwe, J. K. (2014). *How US Evangelicals Are Shaping Development in Uganda.* Aljazeera. Available from: www.aljazeera.com/indepth/opinion/2014/07/us-evangelicals-uganda-2014724135920268137.html [accessed 29 October 2020].

Bishop, S. (2016). Troubling Essentialism: Studying Religion and Feminism. *The Religious Studies Project.* Available from: www.religiousstudiesproject.com/2016/10/13/troubling-essentialism-studying-religion-and-feminism/ [accessed 14 October 2017].

Bradley, T. (2011). *Religion and Gender in the Developing World: Faith-Based Organizations and Feminism in India.* London: I. B. Tauris.

Clarke, G. (2007). Agents of Transformation? Donors, Faith-Based Organisations and International Development. *Third World Quarterly*, 28(1): 77–96.

Clarke, G., Jennings, M., and Shaw, T. (2008). *Development, Civil Society and Faith-Based Organizations: Bridging the Sacred and the Secular.* London: Palgrave Macmillan.

Conroy, J. (2015). Religious Literacy in Higher Education. In A. Dinham and M. Francis (eds.), *Religious Literacy in Policy and Practice.* Bristol: Policy Press.

Deneulin, S., and Rakodi, C. (2011). Revisiting Religion: Development Studies Thirty Years on. *World Development*, 39(1): 45–54.

Dinham, A. (2016). *What Is Religious Literacy? – Q&A with Adam Dinham.* Available from: www.onreligion.co.uk/what-is-religious-literacy-qa-with-adam-dinham/ [accessed 1 June 2018].

Dinham, A. (2017). Religious Literacy in Public and Professional Settings. In B. R. Crisp (ed.), *The Routledge Handbook of Religion, Spirituality and Social Work.* New York: Routledge.

Dinham, A., and Francis, M. (2015). *Religious Literacy in Policy and Practice.* Bristol: Policy Press.

Dinham, A., Francis, M., and Shaw, M. (2017). Towards a Theory and Practice of Religious Literacy: A Case Study of Religion and Belief Engagement in a UK University. *Religions*, 8(276).

Dinham, A., and Lowndes, V. (2008). Religion, Resources and Representation: Three Narratives of Engagement in British Urban Governance. *Urban Affairs Review*, 43(6): 817–845.

Hefferan, T. (2015). *Researching Religions and Development.* In E. Tomalin (ed.), *The Routledge Handbook on Religions and Global Development.* London and New York: Routledge.

Imam, A., Gokal, S., and Marler, I. (2017). The Devil Is in the Details: A Feminist Perspective on Development, Women's Rights, and Fundamentalisms. *Gender and Development*, 25(1): 15–36.

Jeavons, T. (2004). Religious and Faith-Based Organizations: Do We Know One When We See One? *Nonprofit and Volunteer Sector Quarterly*, 33(1): 140–145.

Khalaf-Elledge, N. (2020). "It's a Tricky One" – Development Practitioners' Attitudes Towards Religion. *Development in Practice*, 30(5): 660–667.

McGuire, M. (2008). *Lived Religion: Faith and Practice in Everyday Life.* New York: Oxford University Press.

Moore, D. (2007). *Overcoming Religious Literacy: A Cultural Studies Approach.* New York: Palgrave Macmillan.

Moore, D. (2015). Diminishing Religious Literacy: Methodological Assumptions and Analytical Frameworks for Promoting the Public Understanding of Religion. In A. Dinham and M. Francis (eds.), *Religious Literacy in Policy and Practice.* Bristol: Policy Press.

Moore, D. (2017). *Religion, Conflict and Peacebuilding.* Boston: Harvard Divinity School Module.

Prothero, S. (2007). *Religious Literacy: What Every American Needs to Know – And Doesn't.* San Francisco, CA: HarperSanFrancisco.

Schnable, A. (2016). Frames, Modes of Action, Networks: What Religion Affords Grassroots NGOs. *Journal for the Scientific Study of Religion*, 55(2): 216–232.

Sharafeldin, M. (2013). Egyptian Women's Rights NGOs: Personal Status Law Reform Between Islamic and International Human Rights Law. in Z. Mir-Hosseini, K. Vogt, L. Larsen, and C. Moe (eds.), *Gender and Equality in Muslim Family Law.* London: I. B. Tauris.

Tadros, M. (2010). *Faith-Based Organisations and Service Delivery: Some Gender Conundrums.* Geneva: UNRISD.

Tomalin, E. (2007). *Gender Studies Approaches to the Relationships Between Religion and Development*. RaD Working Papers Series 4. Birmingham, UK: University of Birmingham.

Tomalin, E. (2011). *Gender, Faith and Development*. Oxford: Oxfam.

Tomalin, E. (2012). Thinking About Faith-Based Organisations in Development: Where Have We Got to and What Next? *Development in Practice*, 22(5–6): 689–703.

Wright, A. (1993). *Religious Education in the Secondary School: Prospects for Religious Literacy*. London: David Fulton.

5 Fulfilling the promise of GAD

Addressing religion in gender analyses

This chapter explores how religion can be integrated into the gender analysis phase of development projects. Currently, gender analyses are often conducted via quick desk research, without field interviews, and *after* partnerships are already formed. Comprehensive and concept-based gender analyses can illustrate the links of religion and gender in a given locality, inform project designs, clarify gender needs, and improve the selection of religious partners.

This chapter begins by discussing the downsides of making religion a separate category in gender analysis frameworks. I argue that such a category will likely result in adverse or at least unsatisfactory effects in the current policy environment. Religion is so deeply interconnected with other social forces that a separate category for it might create illusions of fixed boundaries and causal relationships. Instead, a focus on the dynamic forces and power structures surrounding religion and gender is needed. In other words, the shift from WID to GAD must be completed. If GAD was fully implemented to its original intent, a category for religion would likely be redundant. I situate this discussion in post-structural feminist literature, particularly focusing on theories of power, gender performance, and gender policing. My research finds that an analysis of these themes is particularly useful in deconstructing the complex root causes of norms that are often labelled 'religious' and overlooked conceptually.

This chapter introduces a gender analysis tool that practitioners can use alongside their gender approaches to visualise the complex power structures within a particular context that underpin the interplay of religion and gender. It is the first gender analysis tool that centres around power. The tool is illustrated by four examples, each focusing on a predominant GAD theme: female genital mutilation[1]; child, early, and forced marriage; reproductive health access restrictions; and gender-discriminatory laws.

DOI: 10.4324/9781003112549-6

No need for a religion category in analysis frameworks

At the outset of this research, I hypothesised that the integration of religion as a category of analysis into gender analysis frameworks may be a possible solution to bridge the current gap of conceptualising this nexus. However, my research findings suggest that a category for religion is not tenable for two reasons. First, the gap between theoretical and practical gender analyses as outlined previously makes it hard to envision the inclusion of an additional category into frameworks that are already barely applied. Second, development practitioners seem overwhelmed by the challenge of addressing religion in development. A category labelled 'religion' could alienate the study of this subject even further rather than stimulating an in-depth conceptual discussion of it. My findings suggest that development practitioners are already too quick to lump gender norms together as 'religious' and deem them static, ahistorical, and politically risky to engage with as a result. For example, the fact that the Taliban in Afghanistan restrict women's voting rights, among others, could be miscategorised as a religious norm. A closer look, however, reveals the Taliban's deeply patriarchal and political interests for imposing brutal restrictions. Restricting women's voting rights is in no way a uniquely religious pattern. The power structures imposed by the Taliban are somewhat reminiscent of the many women's suffrage movements and their violent oppositions in Western countries themselves. There was a time in the West, too, where it was widely believed – for a variety of reasons – that women have no place in politics. This belief was so normalised that women who tried to challenge it were imprisoned, tortured, or killed.

My conclusion with regards to a category for religion echoes religious studies scholars' standpoints on this question. For example, Arnal and McCutcheon (2013: 28) emphasise the need of 'deconstructing the category [of religion] and analysing its function in popular discourse', rather than 'assuming that the category has content'. Sociologists have criticised the idea of religion as a separate category as it would disregard that religion is an integral part of all aspects of life (Woodhead and Catto, 2012: 2). Feminist scholars have argued that a category for religion cannot justly address its intersection with gender. This is because religion has no set boundaries and is embedded in contexts which are themselves fluid. As Bishop (2016: 2) posits, only when understood with nuance, religion can be considered as part of 'the wider matrix of power relations' with which feminist work is concerned. Finally, a separate category for religion in development is likely to experience a similar fate to the category of gender. GAD scholars have repeatedly criticised the isolated and separate treatment of gender rather than acknowledging that it is a cross-cutting issue. A category for religion may become subject to the same power balances of the development sector, which – as Cornwall et al. (2009: 9) argue – have driven feminist thinking to the edge of its discourse. The narrow focus on religion only through external partnerships already constitutes evidence of the marginalisation of the topic.

Shifting to a concept-based gender analysis

I argue that an integrated analysis of religion rooted in gender theory is better equipped to address the religion–gender nexus than a separate category for religion altogether. This is also in line with the perspectives of the women's rights activists in my sample. In 2017, AWID similarly identified 'a sharpened gender analysis' to be the space through which development should address the 'overarching need . . . to engage critically with the rise of religious fundamentalisms' (Imam et al., 2017: 33). As discussed earlier in this book, a concept-based gender analysis is currently not the norm. Analyses rarely reach beyond gender statistics and practical needs. Notably, there are relatively few gender advisors in development practice who have an academic background in gender studies or feminist theories. Many moved into gender positions from roles focused on social development, livelihoods, community outreach, or communication. One research participant, who is the only gender advisor within her organisation that has a degree in gender studies, explained that:

> there is this believe that gender is something we all just know and don't have to study. But there is a need for development practitioners to ground their gender analysis in conceptual understandings of masculinities and femininities.
>
> (Lisa, Gender Advisor, Government Aid Agency)

She added that such a conceptual understanding enables practitioners to 'react flexibly to different contexts' and allows for an evidence-based consideration of religion. It may prompt development practice to better recognise the multi-layered and diverse expressions of gender relations, masculinities, and femininities and how these interact with religious beliefs in a given context.

A new gender analysis tool

Reviewing what is meant by 'gender norms' would be useful before introducing the new gender analysis tool (Figure 5.2). Gender norms are the collective ideas a social group holds about how women and men should be and act. These norms are learnt and internalised early in life. They frequently establish a life cycle of gender socialisation or stereotyping. Here are some everyday situations that indicate internalised gender norms:

> when girls automatically sit down with their legs together. Girls learn early on that their sexuality is dangerous or dirty. It must be controlled and covered at all times. Boys, on the contrary, are allowed to pee in the streets and 'man-spread' their legs on public transport.
>
> . . . when boys are called assertive and girls are labelled aggressive for the same behaviour. Boys are taught to be leaders and girls are taught to be supporters, team players, and peacemakers. Sometimes women in business meetings may feel the need to apologies before talking in order to avoid being called 'bossy': 'maybe that's a silly question' or 'this may be irrelevant, but. . .'.
>
> . . . when a boy tells his mother that he is going out on a date and she asks 'what is her name'? This question signalises an automatic and internalised expectation for people to be heterosexual.
>
> . . . when baby clothes are deeply gendered, both in colour and in print patterns. For example, boy clothes tend to come with a full range of exciting jungle and ocean animals but with little colour variety, while girl clothes are predominately pink and their animal world is mostly restricted to butterflies and unicorns. Soft colours and peaceful animals reinforce the idea of girls as sweet and silent, while strong colours and wild animals teach boys to be loud and aggressive.

These examples are for illustration only. They are simplified versions of some of the most typical gender norms and stereotypes in societies today. Of course, these examples are not exhaustive and vary from context to context. Sometimes gender norms are so subtle and normalised that it can take a lifetime to realise and unlearn them. This invisibility makes it even more difficult to identify the role religions may play in shaping gender norms.

Gender norms and religious beliefs exist in the same complex power structures and are both subject to change. Both gender and religion need to be studied through a framework that recognises their internally diverse nature and deep roots in historic, cultural, and political contexts. To address the religion–gender nexus, a comprehensive gender analysis needs to move beyond labelling norms as 'religious' yet also examine the complex processes of negotiation behind these norms. How did these norms develop? Who is in charge? How are they manifested? How are they performed? Who polices the norms? Religious labelling without asking such questions obscures the 'messy' power structures behind them. As Sen et al. (2007: 28) argue, gender 'norms reflect and reproduce underlying gendered relations of power'. Norms can entitle people in society by granting them special privileges. But they can also marginalise people by 'normalising shame, inequality, indifference or invisibility' (Sen et al., 2007: 28).

The gender-power analysis tool introduced in this chapter helps expose the complicated and often invisible power structures behind gender norms and highlights how these norms are performed and policed in everyday life. The tool presumes that gender norms are more often a function of power than religion (see Figure 5.1). It does not intend to deny the role religion

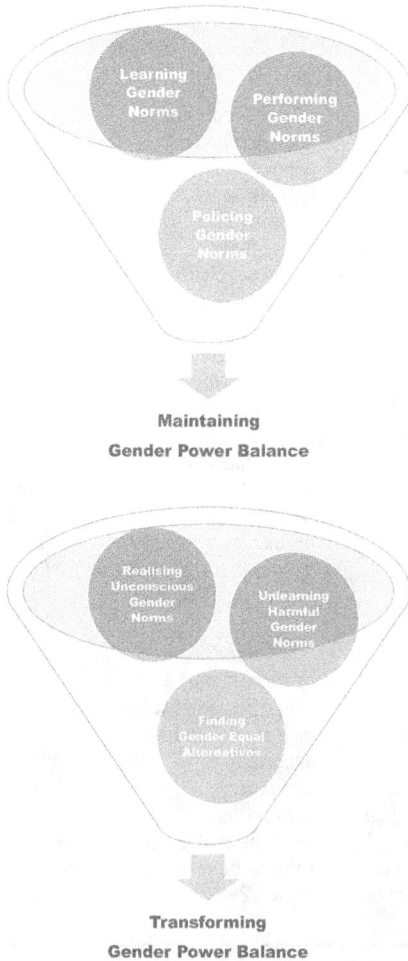

Figure 5.1 Maintaining and Transforming the Gender Power Balance

plays in shaping gender norms but rather illuminate the interplay of the two and the power dynamics that underpin this interaction.

The new gender-power analysis tool consists of a series of questions that enable practitioners to identify whether and how the issue at hand (a gender norm, law, practice, etc.) functions to produce, reproduce, or enforce power structures (see Figure 5.2). It can be used in conjunction with other existing

Learning gender norms and **producing** *power structures*	**Performing** *gender norms and* **reproducing** *power structures*	**Policing** *gender norms and* **enforcing** *power structures*
Does this gender norm/ issue/practice/law. . .	Does this gender norm / issue/practice/law. . .	Is this gender norm/issue/ practice/law. . .
• perpetuate prevalent gender norms? • privilege men over women, or heterosexuality over homosexuality? • give authority to men and fathers over women and children? • devalue one gender? *(e.g., calling grown women 'girls', tipping midwives double if it is a boy, or blaming victims of sexual violence)*	• mirror predominant gender roles? • connect to the idea of honour, modesty, or virginity? • imply that one gender exists in relation to the other? *(e.g., person titles that change for women before and after marriage but stay the same for men such as Miss to Mrs?)* • grant leaders extra political power or votes when they invoke, promote, or advocate for it?	• a punishment for non-conformity? • a reaction to a sudden increase in women's rights or gender equality? Do the 'policers' feel threatened by changes in gender roles? • restricting people's rights to self-determination? Does it only do so for one gender? • a form of controlling or supressing female/ male sexuality? *(e.g., FGM, abstinence-only education, or purity rings)*
Discussion:	*Discussion:*	*Discussion:*
When did this norm/ issue/practice/law originate? What context was it born out of? What are the expected behaviours for women and men? Do they stand in opposition to one another or exist on a spectrum?	Does the performance of this practice cause physiological or physical harm according to survivors? Is it important to adhere to traditional gender roles to be respected in society?	How are gender norms enforced by families, societies, and the state? Who polices who? What are the negative outcomes of this policing?

Figure 5.2 Gender-Power Analysis Tool

gender analysis tools. If a majority of the questions can be answered with 'yes', then the issue at hand is likely a mechanism to maintain a larger system of power. The tool also includes a few non-polar questions to allow space for more rigorous and qualitative analysis.

Gender-Power Analysis Tool

In the following, I provide a review of the feminist literature on power, gender performance, and gender policing that informed the development of this analysis tool. I use the example of female genital mutilation (FGM) for illustration. FGM was named by many research participants as a practice frequently invoked on religious grounds. Later on, I demonstrate how to use the tool in the context of other GAD issues.

Power and gendered religion

As previously discussed, religion and power are deeply entangled. Religions *exist in* and *consist of* power structures. This link has been explored exhaustively in sociology and philosophy (e.g., Weber, 1963; Marx, 1976; Beckford, 1983; Woodhead, 2007). The tool introduced in this chapter builds on this literature to demonstrate how systems of power like patriarchy seek to appropriate religion to legitimise existing power structures and maintain gender imbalances. Virtually all gender norms labelled as 'religious' by participants in my research can be understood as products of such power structures. This demonstrates the strong link between power, religion, and gender. Although sociologists find that 'gender is inseparably bound up with the unequal distribution of power in society' (Woodhead, 2007: 554) and even though development scholars have long argued that 'gender relations are fundamentally power relations' (Cornwall, 1997: 8), the dimension of power is currently not part of any exciting theoretical gender analysis framework. The only framework that briefly addresses power is Kabeer's (1994) Social Relations Approach, in which she poses the questions 'who decides' and 'whose interests are served'. Yet, it does not ask what social norms legitimise and maintain this power; where this power originates; or how it is negotiated, internalised, naturalised, or contested.

Sociology offers a vast collection of discussions around power, much of which is concerned with gender and religion. This literature illustrates how the religion–gender nexus may conceal and maintain predominant power structures. How religion legitimates power has been contemplated since the origin of sociology. To Marx, religion is a reflection of social inequality. In his theory, religion operates like an 'opium of the people' masking the real sources of their oppression, which according to Marx are the exploitive structures of capitalism (Marx, 1976). Religion thus serves as a sanctuary from the harshness of everyday life. Marx further argued that religion teaches non-resistance to oppression and thus cannot generate social change. Instead, religion serves the ruling class to maintain their power and status (Marx, 1976). Weber conceptualised religion as slightly more fluid. According to him, religion could both legitimise power structures *and* generate social change (Weber, 1963). He was interested in how religion constructs and legitimises authority, including systems of 'traditional authority'.[2] Weber argued that traditional authority is embedded in patriarchal systems in which males hold political leadership, moral authority, social privilege, and property control. Modern-day sociology also examined the role religion plays in upholding gendered power relations within a society. Woodhead (2007: 7) argues that it is impossible to disentangle the full complexity of these 'gender orders', but that religion can be a fundamental part of them (also see Sultana, 2012: 4). Woodhead (2007: 7) identifies multiple ways in which religion may relate to gender in the context of power distribution ranging from legitimising gender inequality (*confirmatory religion*) to challenging the existing gender order (*challenging religion*). Woodhead's depiction of confirmatory religion is particularly useful for understanding the religion–gender nexus in development. For example, if a society is patriarchal, the religious interpretations that define gender relations within that society will likely also be patriarchal.

In the case of FGM, religion is invoked to legitimise traditional ideals of modesty and virginity. FGM has been at the centre of debates around gender-based violence and religion in academic literature and beyond (Tomalin, 2007). It is often perceived as an Islamic practice, even though it is also widespread in African Christian communities and, in fact, predates Islam. While the exact number of girls and women worldwide who have undergone genital mutilation remains unknown, it is estimated that more than 200 million girls and women alive today have been subjected to the practice across 31 countries (UNICEF, 2019). Female genital mutilation has been labelled a human rights abuse and major health risk by women's rights movements and international bodies, including the United Nations. Despite bans in many countries, the practice continues to be widespread. Scholars argue that this is because it is 'deeply embedded in cultural understandings of sex and womanhood' (Tomalin, 2007: 15). Also, it is believed to be sanctioned by religion and to safeguard family honour by preserving the modesty and marriageability of women (Kelly and Hillard, 2005).

Typically, the government aid agencies interviewed as part of my research either avoid addressing FGM altogether or take an exclusively health-based approach to it. Given its religious connotations, FGM is often deemed too controversial to engage with and thus is repackaged as part of a health intervention. A health approach addresses the harmful consequences of the practice but leaves its root causes untouched. The patriarchal character of this practice remains little examined or understood in development practice. Women's rights activists expressed their frustration about donors' mislabelling FGM as a religious or even as a cultural practice:

FGM is just pure patriarchy . . . men controlling women's bodies . . . FGM is all about preserving modesty. That is what donors don't understand. No health argument in the world will be effective so long as FGM is seen as the only way to preserve a girl's modesty.

(Salma, Moroccan women's rights activist)

Another women's rights activist added:

FGM is only branded as religious . . . because [religion] is a very very strong force that can accommodate anything and, especially in the case of illiterate people, religion is just the easiest way to communicate.

(Sherine, women's rights activist, Egypt)

Both activists described FGM as guaranteeing virginity in a patriarchal society. Virginity ensures modesty, which allows girls to get married and attain their position, honour, and respect in society. To tackle FGM successfully, its underlying patriarchal power structures must be unmasked. Monagan (2010: 160) considers FGM 'much the same as foot-binding and breast ironing and corsetry . . . carried out by women for the benefit of men'. It is one of the many ways in which the 'the invisible hand of patriarchy' controls female bodies and sexuality (Monagan, 2010: 160). Notably, women may equally assume patriarchal power, enact patriarchal norms, and support patriarchal interpretations of religion (Tomalin, 2007: 18). FGM, for instance, is carried out by women and largely considered the business of women (Monagan, 2010). Both men and women can benefit from the power that comes from upholding normative constructions of gender. As one women's rights activist told me:

When you are a woman in a patriarchal society and you want power, you will stand on the podium of patriarchy and oppress other women wherever you can.

(Nabila, women's rights activist, Malawi)

She mentioned several examples, including the shaming of women or the abuse some women face from their mothers-in-law. Such mothers-in-law may appear powerful, but the power they hold over their daughters-in-law is derived entirely from the patriarchy that values sons over daughters. Women who uphold male dominance become the gatekeepers of patriarchy (Sultana, 2012).

Performing gender roles

Gender roles are the lived expressions of ideas of masculinity and femininity. The construction and performance of these ideas are key ways in which societal power structures are preserved, normalised, and legitimised on an everyday basis (Butler, 1990). Through repetitive performance, binary gender roles mirror existing power structures. For example, male headship and female submission within a family unit mirrors the overall patriarchal nature of a society. Butler (1988) therefore considers gender as 'performative'. She coined her idea of 'gender performativity' following de Beauvoir's claim that 'one is not born, but rather, becomes a woman' (de Beauvoir, 1952; Butler, 1988: 519). Butler considers the gendered body a 'historical situation' that is created through repetitive behaviour rather than a natural fact (Butler, 1988: 521).

The factors that shape gender roles – encouraging some gendered behaviour over others – are highly context specific, diverse, and subject to change. Nevertheless, gender performances, especially of religious women, often come to be seen as purely religious. For example, wearing a headscarf is often described as religious behaviour. Such across-the-board labelling fails to recognise the ambiguity surrounding veiling in religious scripture nor the complex sociocultural circumstances that have influenced whether or not women wear it.

A women's rights activist argues that:

> calling it a religious or even a cultural traditional practice can be problematic because there are places in the world where it wasn't ever religious or cultural. In some places it's only become dominant recently.
>
> (Marlene, women's rights activist, UK)

She explained that even if it appears that in some countries it is common for women to be fully covered today, this may not have been the case in the past: 'today it's a black *Abaya*, 50 years ago it was short colourful dresses'. Therefore, referring to garments as 'religious' would be historically inaccurate. Attributing gender performances to a perceived ahistorical religion is dangerous in the sense that it sacralises these practices and falsely deems them unchangeable. Claiming that gender roles are ahistorical also plays into the narratives of fundamentalist around the globe.

Development practitioners need to understand gendered behaviours as manifestations of power structures that can be subject to change, rather than as static phenomena. What some may generalise as 'religious' is more often an expression of deeply rooted power dynamics that can be found across all societies. Calling these gender norms 'traditional' or 'cultural' is equally problematic. As Nussbaum (1999) has long argued, power relations are typically disguised by traditional gendered practices.

According to a research participant, the reason why development practitioners struggle with interpreting gendered behaviour in religious contexts is that 'they just really don't understand basic concepts of femininity and masculinity and how they are all just socially constructed'. Development practitioners must approach the interplay of religion and gender in so-called 'developing' countries with the same nuance they would apply in 'developed' countries. For example, a gender expert from Indonesia, Nadine, observed that her European colleagues overtly connected any behaviour of Indonesian women to 'how Islamic the country is'. Development's gravitation towards easy answers for intersectional issues might result in simplifications and misrepresentations that practitioners would not tolerate in their own contexts. Such narratives further strengthen the false dichotomy of developed versus developing countries.

Gender policing

So far I have outlined how power structures preserve gender norms, how gender performances normalise these norms, and how religion can be employed to sacralise and legitimates them. I now focus on how these norms are policed on an everyday basis. Gender policing is the act of punishing those who do not conform to gender norms in an effort to maintain the social order (Butler, 1990). It is the way in which 'a social group claims, and sustains, a leading and dominant position in a social hierarchy' (Jackson-Lears, 1985). Gender policing shows what the prevalent gender norms are in a society and who holds power over whom.

Gender policing can be overt and direct, such as in the case of gender-discriminatory laws. But often, gender policing is subtle, normalised, and hard to pinpoint. People might be punished through social alienation or name-calling. Girls may be bullied for appearing 'too masculine', or boys, for behaving 'too feminine'. Likewise, calling boys 'sissy' or girls 'bossy' is an attempt to correct the behaviour that does not conform to dominant gender roles. Punishing a boy for crying is a form of gender policing in any society that considers *real* men to be emotionless. Gender policing is not always verbal. It can also refer to what Lloyd describes as 'normative violence'. This is the type of violence that 'constitutes and regulates bodies according to normative notions of sex, gender, and sexuality' (Lloyd, 2013: 818). For example, sexual harassment of girls whose appearance is deemed immodest can be considered a form of gender policing. Another example is sexual violence against LGBTI people and physically and emotionally traumatising 'gay cures' or 'conversion therapies' (Haldeman, 2002). Normative violence regulates and maintains gender orders and is therefore a key element in the process of reinforcing and naturalising structural inequality (Boesten, 2014).

The practice of FGM could be primarily conceived as a form of gender policing. It censors and controls female sexuality and thereby enforces the prevalent gender norm of modesty. But FGM as a practice is also policed. Girls who have not undergone FGM in a community where it is predominant often suffer discrimination and are described as 'dirty', 'immodest', or 'immoral', according to women's rights activists in my research. Gender policing is so powerful in the case of FGM because of the 'the values, ideologies, and the politics attached to the practice' (Abusharaf, 1995: 53). Feminist literature has warned against the dangers of categorising these practices as primarily cultural or religious since they are deeply rooted in patriarchal conceptions of 'honour' and 'shame' and serve to maintain power structures and control of women's sexuality (Keyhani, 2013). Since gender norms are learnt and internalised early on, it is not unusual for people to police themselves into their respective gender roles. As Nussbaum (1999: 29) writes:

> the traditions have become so deeply internalized that [women] seem to record what is 'right' and 'natural,' and women themselves endorse their own second-class status.

This recalls Foucault's work on power which analysed the relationship between society and the individual body. It understands power as a fluid and constantly shifting force that emerges from every social interaction. He describes how the power of social norms:

> reaches into the very grain of individuals, touches their bodies and inserts itself into their actions and attitudes, their discourses, learning processes and everyday lives.
>
> (Foucault, 1980: 39)

Gender policing, through a Foucauldian lens, demonstrates how individuals internalise normalised societal rules and self-regulate their bodies accordingly. This self-discipline and the power societal pressures hold over individual bodies is what Foucault calls 'biopower' (Foucault, 1977: 140). Biopower is always linked to what is understood to be 'true' in a given time and space.

The complex power dynamics of such practices have not been sufficiently examined by development practitioners. There is a need for development practitioners to uncover and understand instances of gender policing or gender performance rather than simply attributing them to religious practices. Such simplifications also misdirect development's response efforts. They falsely imply the possibility of easy and transferable fixes and result in ill-fitting project approaches and partners. For example, in the case of FGM, a thorough gender analysis would highlight the normative pressure and patriarchal underpinnings of the practice, rendering a health-only-approach insufficient. The social stigmatisation of 'uncut' girls alone is a clear indicator that FGM requires more holistic approaches.

Pathways to change in the case of FGM

Analysing FGM across the concepts of power, performance, and policing illuminates opportunities for change. The analysis tool reveals that FGM at its core is a mechanism to preserve modesty and guarantee marriageability of girls. Many development initiatives focus on disseminating information about the health risks associated with FGM in an attempt to discourage the practice. Other approaches outlawed FGM. For example, Egypt banned the practice in 2007. Nevertheless, an estimated 92% of women and girls still undergo it (UNFPA, 2014). Similarly, in 2019, Somali religious leaders urged politicians to pass legislation that would outlaw FGM and punish offenders. However, many elected officials failed to criminalise the practice for fear of losing the votes of those who continue to believe FGM is a religious requirement (Ajiambo, 2019). Both health and legal approaches are necessary but not sufficient for eliminating FGM. This is because these approaches ignore the powerful social underpinning of the practice. The practice will prevail so long as societies value girls based on their modesty and marriageability and FGM is seen as the only mechanism to ensure it. Simply outlawing FGM will more likely drive the practice underground unless the ban is accompanied by continuous community involvement and a publicity campaign that spreads the message into remote areas where FGM is most common (Parsitau, 2018). One of the women's rights activists in my research concluded that the only long-term solution would be to either alter the concept of feminine modesty or establish alternative pathways to achieve it. But first and foremost, there is a need to de-sanctify the practice and thus weaken the power it holds over people's lives. Religious leaders have been playing an essential role in correcting religious misconception surrounding FGM. For example, a Somali Sheikh has led a campaign for the past eight years, advocating against the practice through sermons at mosques and in local media. Change only happens slowly because 'uncut' girls continue to be stigmatised. Nevertheless, Hassan remains determined to rally religious leaders and politicians to wipe out the practice: 'it's against the Islamic teachings and I will continue to tell people the truth wherever I go to end the practice' (Ajiambo, 2019).

How to use the tool for other GAD issues

The analysis tool can be used to identify the complex power structures behind gender issues that were previously assumed to be purely religious. The tool is designed for practitioners' self-education about the religion–gender nexus in their own contexts, their understanding of other contexts, and as a workshop tool to use with development project participants. Ideally, no practitioners would attempt to address a gender issue without first consulting all the questions in the analysis tool.

To avoid generalisations, this tool is the most effective when the context is as specifically defined as possible. For example, are we addressing a town, a country, or a national law? And is the issue explored in today's time? Is it taking place in a humanitarian crisis, a natural disaster, a conflict state, a global pandemic, or perhaps under emergency law? The occurrence of any of these factors critically impacts gendered and religious dynamics. In some situations, it may be difficult or even impossible to determine which and how circumstances have shaped gender norms. But at the very least, practitioners need to recognise that a) gender norms are in fact context specific and influenced by sociopolitical factors and b) this influence is almost always temporary.

The tool can be applied to any GAD theme, including sexual and reproductive health, gender-based violence, gender-discriminatory legislation, or LGBTI rights. Alongside FGM, these areas are some of the most prominent areas in which the religion–gender nexus emerges. In the following, I demonstrate how to use the tool in the case of child marriage, anti-abortion laws, and gender-discriminatory family laws.

Child, early, and forced marriage (CEFM)

While the global rate of child marriage has declined over the past decade, approximately 12 million girls under 18 are still married each year (UNICEF, 2020). Child, early, and forced marriage (CEFM) results in lifelong – sometimes intergenerational – physical, emotional, material, and psychological consequences. CEFM victims are at significantly higher risk of suffering complications in pregnancy and childbirth, contracting HIV/ AIDS, leaving school, and living in poverty compared to their peers. CEFM also increases the risks of experiencing domestic violence and severely curtails victims' decision-making power and freedoms. Boys can also be victims of CEFM at a prevalence roughly one-fifth that of girls (UNICEF, 2014).

Traditionally, development research connected CEFM to both poverty and religion. However, using the aforementioned analysis tool strongly suggests that CEFM functions as a mechanism to preserve patriarchal power structures. Recent research supports this conclusion. For example, a 2018 Girls Not Brides report connects the root causes of child marriage primarily to patriarchy. Other studies similarly found that CEFM is almost always linked to issues of power, patriarchy, and sexuality, which, in turn, may be shaped by conservative religious interpretations (Lai et al., 2018, in Le Roux and Palm, 2018). These patriarchal beliefs restrict girls to domestic and reproductive roles, control their sexuality, and commodify them during marital exchanges (Boender, 2018; Le Roux and Palm, 2018). The case of CEFM is similar to the case of FGM in the sense that conservative actors continue to perpetuate it. Leaders around the world have cited religion as a justification for not changing laws applicable to child marriage (Greene et al., 2015). For example, research in Bangladesh found that religious leaders have a history of protesting national laws that ban or restrict child marriage (Huda, 2018). Similarly, in the United States, a high-profile Republican congressman vetoed a bill that would have banned child marriage in his home state. He argued that 'it would conflict with religious customs' (Buncombe, 2017). Rather than assuming a fixed causal relationship between CEFM and religion, the analysis tool prompts practitioners to ask, 'Why and how are these two connected?'. The Network Girls Not Brides and Stellenbosh University produced a useful resource detailing why religious leaders continue to promote CEFM (Le Roux and Palm, 2018: ii). The report acknowledges that child marriage occurs in countries around the globe. It focuses specifically on evidence from the 20 countries with the highest CEFM rates, including India, Brazil, Nigeria, Ethiopia, and Bangladesh. In these countries the following patterns were overserved:

- Christianity, Islam, and Hinduism all have sacred texts that have been interpreted in different ways to support forms of child marriage.
- Child marriage upholds and manifests patriarchal power. Marriage and family continue to be central issues wherever religious interpretations have ordained men as natural authorities. CEFM keeps fathers in powerful positions since it re-enforces patriarchal societal structures. In many countries, fathers continue to have the final say about when and who to marry his daughters to.
- Since marriages continue to be seen as an integral social institution across religious groups, weddings constitute religious ceremonies. The role of arranging weddings often forms part of religious leaders' social function, visibility, and identity within their communities. In fear of losing this, some religious leaders may resist increased political and legal regulation of marriage.
- Religious leaders promote what they perceive to be the advantages of child marriage, but they are often out of touch with the negative consequences of it. Their endorsement of the practice is driven by fear and condemnation of premarital sex and pregnancy. Child marriage is often seen as the only solution to these issues. Taylor et al. (2019) found that in Brazil religious leaders promote marriage as the only way to 'sanctify' earlier sin and preserve the 'salvation' of girls in particular. So long as sex outside marriage is considered a sin and female purity is glorified in religious interpretations, child marriages will continue (Taylor et al., 2019). In fragile, high-risk or conflict-ridden spaces, parental fear for children's safety can escalate. For example, fear of sexual violence in refugee camps can lead parents to see child marriage as a form of protection. This fear is fuelled by the powerful taboo around sex that is preserved by conservative voices.
- Social change, especially an increase in women's rights, can lead to religion becoming a dominant and conservative identity marker. When social change is perceived as an attack on religious values, religious interpretations can become increasingly fundamentalist to preserve traditional structures. Women, girls, and female sexuality become a principal site of enforcing the religious character of a community (Katz, 1995). As a result, child marriage can intensify. While rights activists seek to weaken the link between CEFM and religion, those benefitting from it will likely try to strengthen it. For example, a senior political senator in Nigeria who married a 13-year-old girl later called one of his opponents 'un-Islamic' for criticising him (Greene et al., 2015).

Causes for CEFM are diverse and context dependent. The analysis tool can help deconstruct that complexity. In many cases, CEFM becomes a coping mechanism for perceived risks and a preserver of patriarchal power. Religious interpretations may attempt to sanctify and legitimise child marriage. However, labelling CEFM 'religious' obscures the real power struggle behind the practice, which may be about control of women's bodies, political power, or access to resources.

CEFM is linked to the systematic undervaluing of girls in society, and there are no easy fixes. Necessary structural changes could provoke conservative backlash. Religious leaders also play a crucial role in tackling child marriage, for example, by contextualising and reinterpreting religious verses and by highlighting what religion says about caring for children's welfare and safety (Le Roux and Palm, 2018). They can also verify the age of the bride and groom before conducting a religious marriage ceremony. But rather than outsourcing this work entirely to religious partners, development practitioners also need to do their homework. They need to understand how gender norms are socially constructed and how religion and power interact in upholding CEFM. This is crucial to identifying and supporting people who are already seeking to reform the practice.

Restricted access to safe abortion

According to the United Nations, access to reproductive healthcare is a basic human right and key to achieving gender equality. When women and girls do not have access to sexual and reproductive health services or are unable to make informed decisions over their own bodies, they face greater health risks, become pregnant unintentionally, drop out of school, miss out on job opportunities, and lose the freedom to plan their own futures. Nevertheless, many countries around the world continue to restrict women's access to comprehensive reproductive care and information, including access to contraceptives, sex education, or safe abortion services.

For the purpose of illustration, I refer to the example of anti-abortion laws in the United States. In 1973, the US Supreme Court recognised the constitutional right to abortion in the landmark decision 'Roe v. Wade'. However, since 2010, the US abortion landscape has grown increasingly restrictive as more states have adopted laws hostile to abortion rights. White evangelicals in the United States make up the backbone of today's anti-abortion campaign or 'pro-life' movement. Because of this, anti-abortion sentiments are often attributed to religious values. Nevertheless, the analysis tool discussed previously indicates that the pro-life movement was adopted by white evangelicals as part of a political campaign rather than a religious crusade.

Until the 1980s, Evangelical Christians had not engaged in politics in an organised way. When it came to the issue of legal abortion, they were either ambivalent or even supportive, citing individual health, family welfare, and social responsibility (Balmer, 2014). The landmark Roe v. Wade decision did not compel Evangelical Christians to advocate for criminalising abortions immediately. It took another six years and the skilful leadership of conservative activist Paul Weyrich for Christians to seize on abortion, 'not for moral reasons, but as a rallying-cry to deny President Jimmy Carter a second term' (Balmer, 2014). Weyrich, who coined the phrase 'moral majority', believed that a united religious right could control the political direction of the entire country. What he needed was an issue to unite them that 'was more palatable than the religious right's real motive: protecting segregated schools' (Balmer, 2014). While he could easily rally religious leaders for the cause of defending racial discrimination, he knew that it would be challenging to do so with grassroots evangelicals. In search for a different issue to form a Christian political right, Weyrich joined arms with Christian theologian Schaeffer. Schaeffer is considered by many the intellectual godfather of the United States' religious right. Long before meeting Weyrich, he preached against abortion rights and 'secular humanism' which he feared would leave societies in the 'vortex of moral decay' and lead to the 'eclipse of Christian values' (Balmer, 2014). Schaeffer produced a film series that targeted an evangelical audience and depicted the scourge of abortion in graphic terms, including a scene of plastic baby dolls scattered on the beach (Schaeffer, 2016). To Weyrich, anti-abortion sentiments offered the perfect catalyst for a right-wing political identity that united a Christian voting bloc. Such a coalition of 'single-issue voters' has proven a powerful and enduring election-winning machine for decades. Today, a presidential candidate can secure large parts of the Evangelical voter base by expressing his or her commitment to *life*.

What started as a political catalyst quickly turned into a nationwide movement culminating in what civil rights activists have called a systematic attack on women's rights. Rights activists argue that the anti-abortion campaign has succeeded largely because it plays on and preserves patriarchal gender norms (Filipovic, 2019). Schaeffer's son, who was himself part of initiating the pro-life movement, explains that it was intentionally anti-women because 'misogyny sells' (Schaeffer, 2016). He expressed that he regrets his role in creating the movement. The historical context of anti-abortion views may demonstrate why 'misogyny' might have been a selling point. Around the same time that right-wing leaders began promoting abortion restrictions, women's social roles were changing rapidly. Women's ability to control their own reproduction came with a series of opportunities and freedoms. Women could take more charge of planning their futures and decide when, who, and whether to marry, contradicting 'the whole rightwing Christian project, which was, and remains, thoroughly invested in a nuclear family with a father at the head' (Filipovic, 2019). The early anti-abortion movement portrayed legal access to abortion as destabilising traditional family values. But once these arguments fell out of favour in an increasingly feminist world, the campaign pivoted to focusing on *life* instead (Filipovic, 2019). A 2019 national survey further demonstrates the entrenchment of misogyny in the anti-abortion movement.[3] The findings suggest that 'anti-abortion voters are among the most likely – if not the most likely – segment to hold inegalitarian views' (Supermajority and PerryUndem, 2019: 18).

Studying the origin and history of the anti-abortion movement in the United States – viewed through the aforementioned analysis tool – highlights the connections to politics, power, gender, and religion. This analysis demonstrates why the subject of abortion has received attention by right-wing politicians and voters, why it is deeply intertwined with patriarchal interpretations of religion, and why it is harmful to gender equality. Today, anti-abortion views not only function to unite conservative Christian voters but also preserves traditional gender roles. Anti-abortion laws prey on deep distrust of women and their ability to make the right decisions for their own bodies, lives, and families. According to the patriarchal playbook, someone else ought to make those decisions for them. Additionally, since abortion restrictions disproportionately impact poorer women and women of colour, they also maintain systemic racism. Subsequently, reproductive health restrictions also highlight the need for an intersectional gender analysis as discussed in Chapter 2.

Gender-discriminatory family laws

Discrimination against women and girls remains enshrined in many national laws and is often claimed on religious grounds. Although 189 states have ratified the 1981 'Convention on the Elimination of All Forms of Discrimination Against Women' (CEDAW), many countries still maintain reservations about specific articles of the convention. Over 60% of the 440 recorded reservations are religion based. The CEDAW provisions that have attracted the most religion-based reservations are those that relate to gender equality, marriage, and family relations (Cali and Montoya, 2017: 3). This has been the case in Egypt or Bangladesh, for example. Both countries maintain religious reservations against CEDAW Articles 2 and 16. CEDAW's Article 2 requires countries to condemn and legally protect against discrimination

(UN Women, n.d.). Article 16 is concerned with marriage and family matters:

> States Parties shall take all appropriate measures to eliminate discrimination against women in all matters relating to marriage and family relations and in particular shall ensure, on a basis of equality of men and women:
>
> (a) The same right to enter into marriage;
> (b) The same right freely to choose a spouse and to enter into marriage only with their free and full consent;
> (c) The same rights and responsibilities during marriage and at its dissolution'.

(OHCHR, 1979)

Both Egypt and Bangladesh have argued that ratifying these articles goes against divine law. For example, Egyptian government officials explained that its reservation to Article 16 stems from its:

> respect for the sacrosanct nature of the firm religious beliefs which govern marital relations in Egypt and which may not be called in question and in view of the fact that one of the most important bases of these relations is an equivalency of rights and duties so as to ensure complementary which guarantees true equality between the spouses.

(UN Women, n.d., emphasis added)

On the contrary, other Muslim-majority countries, including Turkey, Yemen, Jordan, Lebanon, and Kuwait have ratified CEDAW without reservations. A look at Egypt's and Bangladesh's colonial history may explain why gender-related laws have assumed such as strong religious character and become considerably more contentious compared to other countries. I illustrate the case of Egypt here.

British colonial rule left a common vestige in occupied countries: legal pluralism (i.e., the coexistence of both secular and religious laws). Maintaining religious laws was a way to ensure both cultural consistency and colonial legitimacy. Colonialism significantly changed most of the traditional system of Islamic law in Egypt, including the destruction of regulated religious institutional frameworks that had produced legal scholarship for centuries (Equitas, 2009: 15). These schools of religious thought were abundant and at the time arguably more dynamic, internally vibrant, and progressive than today (Al-Ali, 2002). In most areas of public life, traditional Islamic law was exchanged by colonial 'secular' legislation. The only laws that retained their traditional character were those concerning family matters, which today collectively form the Muslim Personal Status Law (PSL) (Abu-Odeh, 2004). Colonial officials were not interested in reforming or governing marital relationships. They were more concerned with increasing economic productivity and extracting resource. Family matters were left to traditional – often religious – law. Additionally, the preservation of family laws under traditional rule was seen as a symbol of cultural continuity in the new political order (Tucker, 2008: 65). The PSL, or family law, regulates all family-related matters, including marriage, divorce, maintenance, custody, and guardianship.[4] It determines the legality of establishing and dissolving a family, as well as the relations between its members and the rights and duties they have towards each other. Rights activists have argued that the PSL is a patriarchal manifestation of Islamic law and entails a series of gender-discriminatory stipulations, such as a wife's obligation to obedience, a husband's right to guardianship and unilateral divorce, and a husband's obligation to financial maintenance (Sharafeldin, 2013). Since 1979, the PSL has remained unreformed and continues to provide a source for the patriarchal and systematic subordination of women.

The supremacy of men reflected in the PSL not only is inconsistent with the CEDAW but also contradicts Egyptian's constitutional commitment to equality of all citizens before the law. Consequently, international human rights groups have criticised Egypt for asserting full religious authority to discriminate against women in family matters (HRW, 2014). Islamic feminists have also called out the systematic and deliberate confusion of Islamic law (human-made and open to change) with *Shariah* (divine and eternal). According to rights activists and religious feminists, gender inequality in national family laws does not result from *Shariah* itself but from century-old patriarchal interpretations of Islamic sources that have become normalised over time in Islamic Jurisprudence *(Fiqh)*. Musawah, a global Muslim women's rights movement, produced an accessible advocacy tool explaining the differences between those concepts (Musawah, 2016).

Women's rights movements have had some successes in softening family laws. But they continue to experience setbacks, especially because government officials have a political interest in preserving these laws: it offers them a source of religious legitimacy. For example, former President Hosni Mubarak, who was known for his persecution of religious groups, nonetheless protected the religiously claimed PSL to prove his commitment to Islam and maintain the support of large segments of the population. He even reinstated a stricter version of the law and thereby abandoned most of the rights women had attained since the end of colonialism (Bibars, 1987 in Al-Ali, 2002). The current, post-revolution government under Abdel Fattah el-Sisi has similarly preserved the PSL to avoid igniting religiously power-ful voices in the country. In Egypt, just like in the United States, gender-related legislation has become the main avenue through which religious commitment is asserted and political legitimacy is maintained. However, contemporary development approaches have been slow in addressing such laws, if at all.

A deeper analysis of gender-discriminatory family laws can swiftly reveal their patriarchal roots, as well as their functions to maintain the social sta-tus quo and political legitimacy. This again demonstrates the importance of uncovering the underlying power dynamics of so-called religious practices. Such an analysis is essential to complete the shift from WID to GAD and to identify and highlight marginalised local feminist voices and women's rights activists who work tirelessly to challenge inequality.

Conclusion

This chapter argued that the intersection of gender norms and religion is best dissected by an improved gender analysis: one that is grounded in basic gender concepts and a general understanding of gender theories and ideologies. My research suggests that analysing gender norms across the three lenses of power, performance, and policing is particularly relevant for practitioners to produce a holistic yet nuanced analysis that avoids religious generalisation and simplifications. Prevalent gender norms of a social group are **learnt** early on in life and deeply internalised. Norms become natu-ralised through their everyday **performance**. The performance of gender norms is enforced by members of the social group. Often people uncon-sciously **police** themselves into binary gender roles. This daily enactment reinforces predominant norms and ultimately preserves the overall **power balance** and gender relations within the social group.

Informed by feminist literature on power, performance, and policing, this chapter introduces a new gender analysis tool. The main goal of the tool is to highlight the complexity of gender norms and situate the role reli-gion plays (or does not play) in producing and perpetuating these norms. Completing this tool demonstrates that gender norms are part of a larger power matrix. Religion may visibly mirror or legitimise those power struc-tures, without necessarily being the cause of the power structures. Once we understand what produces and perpetuates gender norms, new pathways for change may emerge.

Practitioners cannot consider religion or gender norms outside of the structures they exist in. Taking a power, performance, and policing lens makes the religion–gender nexus visible. It deconstructs complex gender norms and places them within their larger socio-historical contexts. It also offers insights into how the control of gendered bodies can maintain hierarchical power structures and how religion can be used to sacralise and legitimise them. Finally, it demonstrates that gendered religious power dynamics span all countries around the world, including high-income countries. In the face of rising conservative ideologies, it becomes ever more important to understand the dynamic roles that gender and religion play in asserting and maintaining power structures and constructing gendered realities. Such a conceptual analysis is needed to fulfil the promise of the GAD approach.

Notes

1 While other terms such as 'female circumcision' or 'female genital cutting' are also used, this report uses the term 'mutilation' consciously as it follows human rights discourses on this issue which maintain that this term more accurately describes the reality of the practice from a human rights viewpoint.
2 Weber defined three types of authority: charismatic authority which is derived from the personality and leadership qualities of an individual; legal authority which comes from powers that are bureaucratically and legally attached to certain positions; and traditional authority which is legitimate because it 'has always existed'.
3 The survey divides respondents by their position on abortion, and then tracks their answers to ten questions on gender equality more generally.
4 Egyptian Christians and Muslims have a separate Personal Status Law.

Bibliography

Abu-Odeh, L. (2004). *Modernizing Muslim Family Law, Egypt: The Case of Egypt.* Georgetown University Law Center. Available from: http://scholarship.law. georgetown.edu/cgi/viewcontent.cgi?article=1031&context=facpub [accessed 14–23 June 2018].

Abusharaf, R. M. (1995). Rethinking Feminist Discourses on Female Genital Mutilation: The Case of the Sudan. *Journal of Canadian Women's Studies*, 15(2–3).

Ajiambo, D. (2019). *Somali Sheikh Leads a Seven-Year Campaign to End Female Genital Mutilation.* Available from: https://religionnews.com/2019/02/27/ somali-sheikh-leads-a-seven-year-campaign-to-end-female-genital-mutilation/ [accessed 14–23 June 2020].

Al-Ali, N. S. (2002). *Women's Movements in the Middle East: Case Studies of Egypt and Turkey.* UNRSID Report. Available from: https://eprints.soas.ac.uk/4889/2/ UNRISD_Report_final.pdf [accessed 1–12 May 2018].

108 *How to engage with the religion–gender nexus*

Arnal, W. E., and McCutcheon, R. T. (2013). *The Sacred Is the Profane: The Political Nature of Religion*. New York: Oxford University Press.

Balmer, R. (2014). *The Real Origins of the Religious Right*. History Department. Politico Magazine. Available from: www.politico.com/magazine/story/2014/05/religious-right-real-origins-107133 [accessed 1–12 July 2020].

Beckford, J. (1983). The Restoration of "Power" to the Sociology of Religion. *Sociological Analysis*, 44(1): 11–31.

Bishop, S. (2016). Troubling Essentialism: Studying Religion and Feminism. *The Religious Studies Project*. Available from: www.religiousstudiesproject.com/2016/10/13/troubling-essentialism-studying-religion-and-feminism/ [accessed 14 October 2019].

Boender, C. (2018). *Child, Early and Forced Marriage: Care's Global Experience*. CARE. Available from: https://resourcecentre.savethechildren.net/authors/boender-carol [accessed 14 October 2020]

Boesten, J. (2014). Inequality, Normative Violence and Liveable Life: Judith Butler and Peruvian Reality. In P. Drinot (ed.), *Peru in Theory*. London: Palgrave Macmillan.

Buncombe, A. (2017). New Jersey Governor Refuses to Ban Child Marriage Because 'It Would Conflict with Religious Customs. *The Independent*. Available from: www.independent.co.uk/news/world/americas/new-jersey-chris-christie-child-marriage-ban-fails-religious-custom-a7735616.html [accessed 19 October 2020].

Butler, J. (1988). Performative Acts and Gender Constitution: An Essay in Phenomenology and Feminist Theory. *Theatre Journal*, 4.

Butler, J. (1990). *Gender Trouble: Feminism and the Subversion of Identity*. London: Routledge.

Cali, B., and Montoya, M. (2017). *The March of Universality? Religion-Based Reservations to the Core UN Human Rights Treaties and What They Tell Us About Human Rights and Universality in the 21st Century*. Geneva: Universal Rights Group.

Cornwall, A. (1997). Men, Masculinities and 'Gender in Development'. *Gender and Development*, 5(2): 8–13. Taylor & Francis, Ltd. on behalf of Oxfam GB.

Cornwall, A., Harrison, F., and Whitehead, A. (eds.). (2009). *Feminisms in Development: Contradictions, Contestations and Challenges*. London: Zed Books.

de Beauvoir, S. (1952). *The Second Sex* (H. M. Parshley, Trans.). New York: Random House.

Equitas. (2009). *Women's Rights in Muslim Communities: A Resource Guide for Human Rights Educators*. Montréal: Equitas – International Centre for Human Rights Education, Directorate General of Human Rights (DG-HAM) of the Indonesian Ministry of Law and Human Rights (MOLAHR). Available from: http://equitas.org/wp-content/uploads/2010/11/research_EQUITAS_Sharia.pdf [accessed 1–16 June 2019].

Filipovic, J. (2019). A New Survey Shows What Really Interests 'Pro-Lifers': Controlling Women. *The Guardian*. Available from: www.theguardian.com/commentisfree/2019/aug/22/a-new-poll-shows-what-really-interests-pro-lifers-controlling-women [accessed 3 August 2020].

Foucault, M. (1980). Truth and Power. In C. Gordon (ed.), *Power/Knowledge: Selected Interviews & Other Writings 1972–1977*. London: Harvester Press.

Foucault, M. (1977). The Political Function of the Intellectual. Translated by C. Gordon. *Radical Philosophy*, 17: 12–14.

Girls Not Brides. (2018). *Child Marriage in Malaysia: Its Relationship with Religion, Culture and Patriarchy*. Available from: www.girlsnotbrides.org/resource-centre/child-marriage-in-malaysia-its-relationship-with-religion-culture-and-patriarchy/ [accessed 19 September 2020].

Greene, M., Rao, A., Perison, S., Rao, A., and Bartel, D. (2015). *Human Rights and the Cultural and Religious Defense of Child Marriage. Finding Middle Ground*. New York: Ford Foundation Center for Social Justice.

Haldeman, D. C. (2002). Gay Rights, Patient Rights: The Implications of Sexual Orientation Conversion Therapy. *Professional Psychology: Research and Practice*, 33(3): 260–264.

HRW. (2014). *Egypt's Obligations Under International Law*. New York: Human Rights Watch. Available from: www.hrw.org/reports/2004/egypt1204/8.htm [accessed 29 September 2020].

Huda, T. (2018). *Banning Child Marriage in Light of Religion*. Daily Star Asia. Available from: www. thedailystar.net/opinion/society/banning-child-marriage-light-religion-1526377 [accessed 25 August 2020].

Imam, A., Gokal, S., and Marler, I. (2017). The Devil Is in the Details: A Feminist Perspective on Development, Women's Rights, and Fundamentalisms. *Gender and Development*, 25(1): 15–36.

Jackson Lears, T. J. (1985). The Concept of Cultural Hegemony: Problems and Possibilities. *The American Historical Review*, 90(3): 567–593.

Kabeer, N. (1994). *Reversed Realities: Gender Hierarchies in Development Thought*. London: Verso Press.

Katz, S. (1995). The Rise of Religious Fundamentalism in Britain: The Experience of Women Against Fundamentalism. *Gender and Development*, 3(1): 42–44.

Kelly, E., and Hillard, P. J. (2005). Female Genital Mutilation. *Current Opinion in Obstetrics and Gynecology*, 17(5): 490–494.

Keyhani, N. (2013). Honour Crimes *as* Gender-Based Violence in the *UK*: A Critical Assessment. *UCL Journal of Law and Jurisprudence*, 2(1): 255–277.

Le Roux, E., and Palm, S. (2018). *What Lies Beneath? Tackling the Roots of Religious Resistance to Ending Child Marriage*. Research Report. Girls Not Brides. Available from: www.girlsnotbrides.org/resource-centre/what-lies-beneath-tackling-the-roots-of-religious-resistance-to-ending-child-marriage-2/ [accessed 3 April 2020].

Lloyd, M. (2013). Heteronormativity and/as Violence: The "Sexing" of Gwen Araujo. *Hypatia*, 28: 818–834.

Marx, K. (1976). Introduction to A Contribution to the Critique of Hegel's Philosophy of Right. In *Collected Works*, vol. 3. New York: International Publishers.

Monagan, S. (2010). Patriarchy: Perpetuating the Practice of Female Genital Mutilation. *Journal of Alternative Perspectives in the Social Sciences*, 2(1): 160–181.

Musawah. (2016). Shari'ah, Fiqh, and State Laws: Clarifying the Terms. *Knowledge Building Brief*, 1. Musawah. Available from: www.musawah.org/resources/

knowledge-building-brief-1-shariah-fiqh-and-state-laws-clarifying-the-terms-en/ [accessed 22 September 2020].

Nussbaum, M. C. (1999). *Sex and Social Justice.* Oxford and New York: Oxford University Press.

OHCHR. (1979). *Convention on the Elimination of All Forms of Discrimination Against Women.* New York: The Office of the High Commissioner for Human Rights [accessed 18 September 2020].

Parsitau, D. (2018). *How Outlawing Female Genital Mutilation in Kenya Has Driven It Underground and Led to Its Medicalization.* The Brookings Institution. Available from: www.brookings.edu/blog/education-plus-development/2018/06/19/how-outlawing-female-genital-mutilation-in-kenya-has-driven-it-underground-and-led-to-its-medicalization/ [accessed 2 September 2020].

Schaeffer, F. (2016). Web Extra: Full Frank Schaeffer Interview. *Full Frontal with Samantha Bee.* Available from: www.youtube.com/watch?v=MhLY0JqXP-s [accessed 24 November 2020].

Sen, G., Ostlin, P., and George, A. (2007). Unequal, Unfair, Ineffective and Inefficient. Gender Inequality in Health: Why it Exists and How We Can Change It. In *Final Report to the WHO Commission on Social Determinants of Health.* Solna: Karolinska Institute.

Sharafeldin, M. (2013). Egyptian Women's Rights NGOs: Personal Status Law Reform Between Islamic and International Human Rights Law. In Z. Mir-Hosseini, K. Vogt, L. Larsen, and C. Moe (eds.), *Gender and Equality in Muslim Family Law.* London: I. B. Tauris.

Sultana, A. (2012). Patriarchy and Women's Subordination: A Theoretical Analysis. *Arts Faculty Journal* (4): 1–18.

Supermajority and PerryUndem. (2019). *Gender Equality, the Status of Women and the 2020 Elections.* Available from: https://int.nyt.com/data/documenthelper/1647-supermajority-survey-on-women/429aa78e37ebdf2fe686/optimized/full.pdf#page=1 [accessed 17 August 2020].

Taylor, A. Y., Murphy-Graham, E., Van Horn, J., Vaitla, B., Del Valle, A., and Cislaghi, B. (2019). Child Marriages and Unions in Latin America: Understanding the Roles of Agency and Social Norms. *Journal of Adolescent Health: Official Publication of the Society for Adolescent Medicine,* 64: S45–S51.

Tomalin, E. (2007). *Gender Studies Approaches to the Relationships Between Religion and Development.* RaD Working Papers Series 4. Birmingham, UK: University of Birmingham.

Tucker, J. E. (2008). *Women, Family, and Gender in Islamic Law.* Cambridge: Cambridge University Press.

UN Women. (n.d.). *Reservations to CEDAW.* Available from: www.un.org/womenwatch/daw/cedaw/reservations.htm [accessed 2 September 2020].

UNFPA. (2014). *Female Genital Mutilation.* UNFPA Egypt. Available from: https://egypt.unfpa.org/en/node/22544 [accessed 5 September 2020].

UNICEF. (2014). *Ending Child Marriage: Progress and Prospects.* New York: UNICEF. Available from: www.unicef.org/media/files/Child_Marriage_Report_7_17_LR.pdf [accessed 25 September 2020].

UNICEF. (2019). *What Is Female Genital Mutilation? 7 Questions Answered.* Available from: www.unicef.org/stories/what-you-need-know-about-female-genital-mutilation [accessed 28 September 2020].

UNICEF. (2020). *Child Marriage Around the World.* Available from: www.unicef.org/stories/child-marriage-around-world [accessed 3 September 2020].

Weber, M. (1963). *The Sociology of Religion.* Boston: Beacon Press.

Woodhead, L. (2007). Gender Differences in Religious Practice and Significance. In J. Beckford and J. Demerath (eds.), *The Sage Handbook of the Sociology of Religion.* London: Sage: 550–570.

Woodhead, L., and Catto, R. (eds.). (2012). *Religion and Change in Modern Britain.* London: Routledge.

6 Tackling the taboo

Transforming practitioners' attitudes towards religion (and gender!)

In contrast to existing literature that presents the development industry as increasingly open to engagements with religions, my research found that practitioners throughout the sector remain uncomfortable with this subject. It appears that the normalisation of secularism coupled with the idea of development practitioners as 'neutral' has rendered Western development organisations significantly religion-blind. Meanwhile, orientalist mindsets reminiscent of colonialism continue to permeate the development sector and essentialise religion as backwards, risky, and a unique feature of the 'developing world'. Contrary to global policy pushes, addressing religion in practice continues to be largely left to individual discretion and practitioners show an overwhelming reluctance to engage. Unfortunately, the same appears to be true for gender, as discussed in Chapter 2.

I concur with Dinham (2017) that any meaningful study of religion must be preceded by a critical reflection on one's preconceived notions and attitudes towards it. This chapter, therefore, illustrates current attitudes towards both religion and gender and contemplates ways forward.

Religion – a 'Trickster' in development?

Despite numerous global faith conferences and external policy pushes, development practitioners' overall attitudes towards religion remain negative and have gone virtually unaddressed by organisations, policymakers, or academic literature. Newley established units within government aid agencies that are tasked with spearheading organisations' turn to religion find themselves challenged daily by these attitudes. For example, Simone, a leader of a subdivision for religious partnerships of a large European government aid agency said that employees are afraid to 'be stirring up a hornet nest' and express significant scepticism and resistance. To address these sentiments, she is primarily focused on 'calming fears' and helping

DOI: 10.4324/9781003112549-7

employees across all departments 'warmup to religion'. Religion is considered 'such a sensitive topic', Simone explained, that 'people believe we should not try and engage' with it in any way. This was a common sentiment among development organisations interviewed. A participant from a large US recipient organisation found that 'people are a little nervous' when it comes to religion and are unsure 'what it has to do with them'. As a result, this organisation, like many others, usually avoids it completely despite acknowledging its importance on paper.

The vocabulary used by development practitioners during interviews when describing religion was often a first indicator of practitioners' scepticism towards it; an engagement with religion was frequently labelled 'risky', 'controversial', 'complicated', 'political', or 'too sensitive'. Meanwhile, partnerships with FBOs were mostly described as a way to 'play it safe'. Notably, the most commonly used initial reaction towards religion was the expression 'tricky':

> *Uuuh, this is a tricky one.* (Ellen, European government aid agency)
> *Well, religion is a tricky one.* (Samantha, North American government aid agency)
> *It's tricky, you know.* (Elizabeth, European government aid agency)
> *It is really tricky.* (Cheryl, US recipient organisation)

From the contexts, it seemed as though 'tricky' referred to 'difficult', 'unclear', or 'complicated'. Moreover, there was a sense of confusion and fear around the subject of religion and a notion that – if mishandled – its volatility can have serious consequences for practitioners' careers and organisations' reputations. The frequent use of the term 'tricky' reminds one of the anthropological notion of 'the Trickster' (see Radin, 1956; Ricketts, 1966; Pelton, 1980). Anthropologists have been fascinated with the mythological figure of the Trickster which frequently appears in folklore as 'a gross deceiver, a crude prankster, . . . and a fool caught in his own lies' (Pelton, 1980: 7). The Trickster's multiple personas and true character have been the source of much debate and confusion. Most attempts have left 'the figure curiously untouched' and have not allowed scholars to come to grips with 'his ambiguity' (Boas, 1898 in Ricketts, 1966: 329). Radin's (1956: 165) description powerfully highlight the complex contradictions the Trickster is believed to contain and exhibit:

> [The] Trickster is at one and the same time creator and destroyer, giver and negator, he who dupes others and is always duped himself. . . . At all times he is constrained to behave as he does from impulses over which he has no control. He possesses no values, moral or social, is at

the mercy of his passion and appetites. . . . He is primarily an inchoate being' who is protohuman.

Development practitioners' portrayals of religions align closely with anthropological notions of the Trickster. Religion is seen as unpredictable, uncontrollable, impulsive, operating outside of norms and civility, and capable of sabotaging development's agenda. The idea of religion as a Trickster may help explain the 'excessive caution', 'fear', and 'nervousness' of development practitioners towards religion.

But how has religion come to earn itself such a reputation?

Women's rights activists interviewed as part of this research overwhelmingly agreed that the reason is a systematic dismissal and lack of knowledge about religion, which over decades has provided ample space for assumptions and misconceptions. On the contrary, many women's rights activists displayed a solid understanding of the sociopolitical role religions play in society and everyday life. Meanwhile, in headquarters of Western development organisations, three assumptions appear to have rendered religion a blind spot on many practitioners' agenda: (1) the notion that development is inherently neutral, (2) the belief that religion and neutrality are mutually exclusive, and (3) the assumption that objectivity is best preserved through secularism.

1   Development's assumption of its objectivity resembles a platonic ideal of objective truth, which lies outside of the human and is independent of personal beliefs (Cratylus 385b2; Sophist 263b in David, 2016). There is a gap between development's idealisation of objectivity and objectivity in reality, which according to contemporary sociologists and philosophers hardly exists (Mill, 1831 in Foucault, 1980; Macleod, 2018). It appears that development practitioners continue to believe that objectivity is not only needed but indeed possible. There is an urgent need for more research examining this gap to identify development practitioners' positionalities and potential biases. Research participants explained that the commitment to objectivity is a key criterion for their organisations' eligibility for funding. Consequently, they frequently stressed the importance 'to stay neutral' and to follow 'a neutral framework', without explaining how they acquired and secured such neutrality in the first place. For example, a North American government aid agency advisor struggled to answer any questions about

religion, explaining that 'it's hard because it does come from having to do a neutral framework'.

2 It is widely assumed that personal religious beliefs conflict with the perceived neutrality of so-called 'secular' development organisations. A participant working for a European government aid agency's subdivision that focused specifically on religious partnerships explained that, after a diversity assessment within his organisation, he was offered confidential feedback by several colleagues. Some expressed 'that when they let people know they had a faith they thought their contribution was treated differently'. He noted that this feedback 'isn't quantifiable, purely anecdotal', but that he was astounded to find out that such attitudes persisted at all. In other organisations, the opposite appeared to be the case. A strict secular framework was not the norm everywhere, especially when it came to gender programming. Participants from a North American government aid agency expressed hesitation when contradicting their agency's own religious values and conservative gender policies. They asked not to be quoted or clarified that some of their views do not represent their professional capacity. A gender advisor from this agency said that if she was to give 'her honest answer' to one of my follow-up questions on the aid agency's religious values and their gender policies, I would have to switch off the voice recorder. A gender advisor from a recipient organisation of this agency made a similar request immediately after praising a religiously liberal organisation that defends women's rights to contraceptives and legal abortion. Participants from these organisations noted the paradox that religion 'in the field' was labelled as suspicious and subjective, while at the same time their own organisations' religious values influenced gender policies. Engagement with *external* religion is still widely considered controversial or biased rather than neutral. This again illustrates the religion-blindness of development, failing to acknowledge practitioners' own biases and the way religion influences the policies of donor governments.

3 Most participants from bilateral aid agencies and their recipient organisations agreed that objectivity is best guaranteed within a secular framework. In other words, adherence to secularism becomes the monitoring mechanism for development's objectivity, while religion is seen as an antithesis to it. Pronouncing secularism as the driver for progressive development is in line with secularisation theory, which gained prominence in the post-war period and has since been exhaustively discussed and debunked by sociologists of religion (Woodhead and Catto, 2012). To assume that secularism is inherently objective obscures its own

subjectivity. That is, the secular is not a neutral space. As Casanova (2009: 13) argues, 'secular neutrality' is a 'myth'. Dinham argues that, as a concept, the secular is just as misunderstood as religion itself (Dinham, 2017: 259). Development's claim of secularism becomes particularly problematic since it neglects the pervasive Christian discourse of colonial-cum-development (Fiddian-Qasmiyeh, 2015). This Christian-centric discourse has still been notable in the post-war development industry as well. Research participants expressed concern about how conservative Christian discourses in donor countries continue to influence their foreign aid policies, for example, in the context of women's reproductive health project or initiatives to combat HIV/AIDS (see Chapter 2).

This reflects Escobar's (2007) critique of development as simultaneously an ideological export and an act of cultural imperialism. According to postcolonial development critique, such cultural imperialism rests on a forged separation between the West as enlightened and the *rest* as backwards and in need of external assistance. While development practitioners' awareness of the influence of religions within their own countries seems disguised by a cloak of secularism, religion in developing countries is painted as regressive, subjective, unpredictable, and a unique feature of developing countries. This representation of religion fosters a dichotomy between the progressive neutral West and the regressive biased rest. In his influential work *Orientalism* (1978), Said argues that Western representations of religion in the so-called Third World are part of a larger project to dominate it. His analysis is useful to make sense of development's idea of tricky religion. He critiques the Eurocentric prejudice and false cultural representations through which the West perceives the East. Said argues that such representation stems from the colonial period in which the West romanticised backward images of Asia in general and the Middle East in particular. The study of the East served as a self-affirmation of European identity, rather than an objective academic study. As a result, oriental studies have functioned as practical methods of cultural discrimination and ultimately served as implicit justifications for Western imperial ambitions. More recently Said (2003: xviii) lamented that such patterns continue to exist and 'the grip of demeaning generalisations and triumphalist cliché in Europe and especially in the US' has in fact tightened. A North American government gender advisor eager to move away from the subject of religion explained that religion is housed within 'a generic social and cultural category'. She maintained that 'it's different from us and that's all I say about that'. In contrast, a former advisor from a different government aid agency was surprised such assumptions still existed:

There is this idea, that we are so advanced and the others are traditional – this dichotomy, this really exists. You would read this sometimes in articles, and it is really the case.

(Lisa, gender advisor, government aid agency)

Lisa argued that there still is a widespread assumption among development
practitioners that they themselves have no religion, gender, or culture and
can, therefore, operate as a 'blank entity'. Frequently invoked expressions
such as 'the Muslim World', in both verbal and written discourses, further
perpetuate this dichotomy and invite homogenisations and generalisations.
It creates the romanticised notion Said was referring to: a world that is internally homogeneous, distant, and bound together by its distinct static and
backward features. Nadine, a field-based gender advisor of a government
aid agency, found herself motivated to study the complexity of lived religion. She started organising informational sessions and repeatedly invited
colleagues from the agency's headquarters to attend. She lamented that
there was little interest unless people saw a way to satisfy their preconceived notions of religion:

We have quite a lot of Islamophobic people in [the donor country], they
often come to Muslim majority countries and would like to have certain
issues confirmed.

Nadine recalled a delegation from the agency's headquarters visiting and
hearing about one of her scheduled seminars on gender and Islam. Many
of them expressed their excitement to attend but were subsequently disappointed when they learnt that the session was on feminist interpretations
of the *Hadith* (sayings of the Prophet). Not understanding what the Hadith
were and confused by the possibility of Islamic feminism, Nadine recalled
the headquarters' delegation 'quickly backing out' and never asked to attend
again. All they wanted, she found, was to see some of their negative stereotypes confirmed like 'all Muslim women are oppressed' and 'Islam is
misogynistic'. Overall, she said, 'the interest in learning about religion is
pretty limited'.

Especially in the context of gender issues, negative preconceptions
about religion run particularly deep. Religion is largely perceived to be an
obstacle to gender equality and quickly put aside. This gendered connota-
tion of religion is not an invention by development practitioners but again
the product of a long colonial tradition of describing the oppression of
women to be integral only to certain non-Western societies (Spivak, 1993;
Abu-Lughod, 2002; Said, 2003; Fiddian-Qasmiyeh, 2015). According to
Said's (2003) work, gender oppression continues to be a prominent theme

ascribed especially to 'backward' Arab and Muslim societies. Abu-Lughod's (2002) work compellingly challenges the idea that Muslim women need to be liberated by the West. She argues that the representation of *Other* women has served justifications for the War on Terror and America's invasion of Afghanistan while simultaneously covering up messy historical and political dynamics that have perpetuated inequality. Current development literature continues to perpetuate the dichotomy between the West as homogenously feminist and secular and developing countries as religious, traditional, and patriarchal. For example, Deneulin and Bano (2009: 162, 165) – although providing useful considerations of the gendered effects of development's secular ideology – repeatedly invoke constructs, such as 'secular liberal traditions' and 'Western secular feminism'. For example, they find that:

> [w]e may not expect an immediate harmony between Western secular feminist and Pakistani Muslim views on what it means for a woman to be empowered.

This not only frames feminism as a Western export but also puts it in contrast to 'Pakistani Muslim views'. It creates two mutually exclusive groups arranged in a hierarchical order reminiscent of the *othering* criticised in postcolonial theory. Equally, Deneulin and Bano's analysis appears to classify women in Muslim countries as either 'Westernised elite' or 'Muslim women' based on how liberal they are. This overlooks the possibility of Muslim women to be liberal and feminist without being Westernised. In other words, one does not cease to be Muslim when one exhibits similar traits to those claimed as Western. Instead, development discourses need to expand their understanding of what it means to be Muslim, which reflects a wide and nuanced spectrum just like any other religious identity. Principles of feminism and liberalism are not Western inventions, likewise, patriarchy and conservativism exist in the West as well and influence its domestic and foreign policies. A good example may be the case of public breastfeeding which is common, legal, and widely accepted across most countries in Africa and the Middle East, while in many Western countries women who breastfeed in public continue to face conservative backlash. Development practitioners' preconceived simplified narratives of religion continue to replace nuanced understandings of religion, including its complicated entanglements in gender politics. It is important to note that these religious simplifications and stereotypes are not limited to Western development organisations. An Indian women's rights activist in my research recalled overhearing some of her local colleagues making statements such as 'at the end of the day they are Muslim girls, how much can we do with them?'. Again, portraying Muslim woman as inherently oppressed covers up the underlying complex historic and sociocultural dynamics that are vital in creating and perpetuating this inequality. Such orientalist representations seem to contradict development's principle of objectivity. I conclude that the real trickiness then lies in navigating this messiness. This entails abstaining from generalisations and orientalist essentialisations, and – as one activist said – address 'the really terrible imperialist dynamics' at home that normalise such representations.

Consequently, Said (2003: xix) distinguishes between two types of knowledge: the knowledge that is based on the 'the will to understand for purposes of co-existence and humanistic enlargement of horizons' and the knowledge which is driven by 'the will to dominate for the purposes of control and external dominion'. The first knowledge is a result of 'understanding, compassion, careful study, and analysis for their own sakes' while the second type of knowledge forms part of 'an overall campaign of self-affirmation, belligerency and outright war'. So long as the discussions around religion are accompanied by an *Othering* mindset, no meaningful engagement with the religion–gender nexus can take part.

Adverse attitudes to gender

The way religion is often ignored by secular-minded development practitioners is in many ways similar to the way gender is dismissed by mainstream development staff who do not consider it relevant to their practice (see Chapter 2). There is a need for research that investigates the attitudinal factors relating to gender in development and to what extent they influence the sidelining of gender issues or the rendering of gender activities as mere checklists. Any attempt to address the religion–gender nexus in development practice needs to be preceded by such an investigation.

Aside from the person assigned to the gender workstream of a project, mainstream staff of development organisations do not typically preoccupy themselves with gender dynamics and if they do, they rarely have the time, know-how, or audience to make an impact. Mainstream staff, in the words of my research participants, often consider gender an additional 'nuisance' they have to 'deal with' (Jennifer, gender advisor, recipient organisation). More than two decades ago, Razavi (1997) already warned of such hostility towards gender. Yet, little has been achieved to address and counteract such attitudes in development practice. Rogers' (2003) *diffusion of innovation* theory explains how new ideas are accepted and implemented in organisations. It could clarify why GAD has been so little adopted. Rogers' theory lays out five stages of innovation processes:

1   knowledge or awareness of an innovation and the potential need for it;
2   persuasion and interest creation;
3   evaluation and decision to adopt the innovation;
4   implementation of the innovation; and
5   confirmation of continuous use of the innovation going forward.

When it comes to gender, it appears that the development industry is jumping to stage 4 (i.e., attempting GAD adoption and gender mainstreaming) before having completed stages 1 through 3. Rogers' theory assumes that people decide on a relatively voluntary basis whether or not to adopt an innovation. This means that by the time adoptees reach the stage of implementation, they fully believe in the innovation. However, this is not the case in development. Stage 1 is met through an industry-wide policy, such as the OECD gender mandate. Gender mainstreaming was institutionalised, regardless of whether individuals committed to it. Stage 2, which would persuade practitioners to subscribe to GAD principles, is still outstanding in the development sector. This creates a divergence: development practitioners who personally are not persuaded by the GAD approach still have to mainstream gender and complete a gender analysis to receive funding. This may explain why gender efforts are often limited to only fulfilling the bare minimum requirements.

If his framework was applied to gender and development, it would likely also show that the *critical mass* needed for the adoption of GAD remains missing. Theoretical GAD ambitions are yet to be translated into practice by a larger number of adoptees to make a difference. Currently, too many 'laggards', as Roger calls them, dominate the industry who are not convinced by the necessity of GAD. Out of the six government aid agencies in my research sample, only two seemed to have achieved gender mainstreaming, or in the words of one of their gender advisors, 'moved beyond a stage where they had to convince development practitioners of the importance of gender' (Ellen, gender director, government aid agency). The importance of GAD has been acknowledged throughout Ellen's organisation, which can now focus exclusively on the implementation phase. All other aid agency participants spoke repeatedly about their daily efforts to convince staff members of the importance of holistic gender approaches. The following sentiments were frequently expressed by participants:

> People don't spend much time on gender. Gender is only a checklist, a superficial desk study at best.
>
> (Nadine, gender advisor, government aid agency)

There is no one here who actually studied gender and who could conceptually understand the gendered dimensions and flexibly apply these [concepts] in diverse contexts.

(Lisa, gender advisor, government aid agency)

There are only two of us within the entire organisation working on gender.

(Amelia, gender advisor, US recipient organisation)

We do a lot of trainings, trying to convince others.

(Cheryl, gender advisor, US recipient organisation)

Gender advisors specifically pointed out the gender-blindness among the senior management of their organisations. This corresponds with Cornwall et al.'s (2009) argument that existing power balances within the wider development arena drive feminist thought to the edge of the discourse. Lisa, a gender advisor of a government aid agency, explains that oftentimes staff's unwillingness to acknowledge their own knowledge gaps obstructs the learning process:

Because gender is considered something that we are already all familiar with, and the higher you go the least likely someone will admit a lack of knowledge or engagement. The people at the very top have the feeling they cannot say 'I have no idea what these gender people just talked to me about'.

The necessity of considering intersectional subjects, such as gender, religion, or race may be difficult to comprehend on a mere rational level. According to gender advisors of multiple organisations, staff may accept the importance of these issues on paper but on a personal level many 'do not care about it because it is not relevant to them' (Claire, gender director, recipient organisation). Claire argued that unless staff have personally experienced what the category of gender means, they are unlikely to advocate for GAD. One government aid gender advisor explained that:

It has to resonate personally, people have to get it in a very personal way and go through a personal transformation to be a real champion for change.

(Elizabeth, gender advisor, European government aid agency)

Other participants similarly felt that people who had experienced little to no discrimination in their lives were typically less receptive to the issue of gender. According to research participants, these were typically senior white men in management positions. By the same token, research participants argued that people who have previously experienced racism or some form of discrimination may be in a better position to understand gender issues in development since they share a personal experience of discrimination. This is reminiscent of Kimmel's influential work on men and gender equality, in particular, his assertion that 'privilege is invisible to those who have it' (Kimmel, 2002). Kimmel finds that those people who are quick to consider categories, such as gender, race, or religion, tend to be those who feel a personal disadvantaged based on these categories in their daily lives.

All this demonstrates the large and persistent gaps between development policy mandates and practice implementations. The gap is driven by a missing stage in the GAD adoption process: persuasion and interest creation. Personal attitudes and biases will remain unaddressed unless development engages with internal change processes as much as it addresses change in foreign countries and outside institutions. Since interest in engaging with religion is also still relatively low, there is little chance that the intersection of both religion and gender will be addressed in the current working environments.

Ways forward

The first step to solving a problem is to identify it. The origins and effects of personal biases have not yet been discussed in development theory. Arguably, the most notable effort to understand biases has been brought forward by the World Bank's (2015) World Development Report. The report does not address religion or gender specifically but is useful in that it brings together the work of psychologists and behavioural economists that expose unconscious biases in people's thinking processes. The final chapter is exclusively concerned with the biases of development practitioners themselves and finds that:

> [d]evelopment professionals can be susceptible to a host of cognitive biases, can be influenced by their social tendencies and social environments, and can use deeply ingrained mindsets when making choices.
> (World Bank, 2015: 181)

According to the World Development Report, these cognitive biases can lead development practitioners to make consequential mistakes impacting the lives of those they ought to help. Tversky and Kahneman (1981) had long argued that cognitive biases are a result of mental shortcuts. According to them, development professionals, just like all human beings, have two systems of thinking: the automatic one and the deliberative one. Instead of performing complex rational calculations every time humans need to make a decision, automatic thinking relies on pre-existing mental models and shortcuts that are incomplete and can lead down the wrong path. Mental shortcuts are based on assumptions humans have created throughout their lives and can stem from their experiences as well as their education. Relying on this literature, the World Development Report offers useful insight into personal biases. Recommendations from the report could easily be applied to practitioners' current engagement and disengagement with religion and gender. Surprisingly, the report was produced in collaboration with several large bilateral government aid agencies, many of which participated in my research study. However, none of the agencies interviewed referenced this report nor did development practice or donor reporting show knowledge of it. This again indicates a large gap between research contracted by government aid agencies and the application and translation of it into practice. The report even recommends that:

> [b]ecause the decisions of development professionals often can have large effects on other people's lives, it is especially important that mechanisms be in place to check and correct for their biases and blind spots.
>
> (World Bank, 2015: 181)

As my findings suggest, such mechanisms are currently nowhere to be found. Furthermore, the absence of a conversation around biases within development practice again shows the one-dimensional nature of development: in the field, development organisations are indeed concerned with changing attitudes and overwhelmingly acknowledge the centrality of people's mindsets to achieving long-lasting progress. This became especially evident in my document analysis which indicated frequent mentioning of beneficiaries' attitudes and mindsets as barriers to development goals, including 'gender equality'. Nevertheless, development practitioners – like people everywhere – are subject to the same biases. There is a need for development organisations to engage in an internal conversation about the deeply rooted biases and attitudes to deconstruct normative mindsets and normalised mental shortcuts.

When it comes to religion, a starting point may be to consider how religion – and the purpose of considering it – is framed. This framing influences practitioners' attitudes towards religion. During interviews, multiple government participants quickly dismissed religious considerations as too risky, assuming the purpose was to change people's beliefs. There was no apparent distinction made between different ways of engaging with religion, for example, studying religion versus adopting religious views versus influencing and changing religious beliefs. When asked about engaging with religion, a participant from a US recipient organisation immediately expressed her nervousness about 'preaching and trying to change people's minds', as though this was the only way religion could be addressed. This reaction was not an isolated incident but a frequent response. A representative of a North American government aid agency stressed several times throughout the hour-long interview that they have to be 'extremely, extremely careful' and aware of their reputation abroad and position as a government agency, which makes any consideration of religion unlikely. To assume that the only way to consider religion is to meddle in it again portrays religion as an inherent obstacle, rather than as a subject which intersects with other development themes and therefore requires analytical consideration just like any other issue. This one-way reformist approach also emphasises a sense of superiority of development agencies over local stakeholders.

At this point, it is worth considering the political context the 1998 'turn to religion' was born into, which in many ways continues to dictate how religion is framed in development today. Development's turn to religion originated in the context of increased political discourses on religious extremism and the War on Terror. The resulting concern with domestic and international security policy gave FBOs a sudden strategic relevance. Deneulin and Rakodi (2011: 46) illustrate how religious groups 'in their more "moderate" guise (particularly in the eyes of Western donors)' are seen as potential bridge-builders and outreach channels to the members of their faith (see also Jones and Petersen, 2011: 1293). A participant in my research who leads a subdivision for religious partnerships in her government aid agency also lamented that religion continues to be largely framed in terms of conflict, instability, or inequality. Several research participants addressed religion exclusively in the context of regions that are currently experiencing conflicts. Afghanistan and Syria were mentioned especially frequent. There is reason to believe that such framing influences practitioners' perspectives on the issue of religion. If the only frame of reference is violence, how else could religion be conceived? Or as Abu-Lughod (2002) theorised in the context of the War on Terror: religion becomes the threat and women the victims.

My call is for a study of religion and gender that echoes Said's ideals of coexistence and enlargement of horizons for the benefit of the greater good. A thoughtful study of religion that produces a conceptual understanding of its connection to other development issues such as gender seems to be a healthy middle path between passive cultural relativism and aggressive Eurocentric imperialism. Considering religion does not necessarily mean taking a direct stance on religious ideas and practices or weighing in on ongoing local religious debates. It means recognising the dynamic debates and diverse voices within any context, and acknowledging the different and changing roles that religions play across all dimensions of life. I do not propose a study such as Prothero's (2007) that attempts to map out the entire theological landscape of religions and their internal traditions. Matters of traditions, belief, and identity are so fluid that there is no *one* way of practising a religion (see Dinham, 2017). Therefore, it is unlikely that one study could adequately capture and portray them all. Rather, I advocate for a study that conceptualises the social constructs and power dynamics *behind* these practices while acknowledging that they are historically situated. A reflective and critical engagement with religion and gender within one's own context may make it easier for practitioners to see that this interaction is indeed a global occurrence and not a 'developing country issue'. It may visualise the context-specific complexity of gender and religion and deconstruct deeply normalised developed/developing country dichotomies. For example, religiously influenced gender norms can be found in countries all over the world, especially when it comes to reproductive health, gender relations, or family matters. If the purpose of considering religion and gender was conducting such an internal conceptual study, current levels of fear and caution may be less justifiable. The necessary time, skills, and enthusiasm for such a study, however, is yet to be discussed in development literature.

It remains to be seen whether and how the development sector will be able to break the power structures that have sidelined gender. There is an urgent need to normalise discussions around gender and feminism. This shift will be driven by people who are both willing and able to champion change within their organisations. More research, theorising change and leadership within the development sector, is required to understand how people can persuade others to adopt GAD principles. I will address some of this in the next chapter. Finally, a few research participants mentioned the need for reflexivity and neutrality training for development practitioners. While there is further research required to assert the practicality and effectiveness of such training, its necessity is apparent and immediate.

Conclusion

The evidence presented in this chapter suggests that attitudes of development practitioners are underexamined while effectively driving and determining policy and practice concerning the religion–gender interface. The evidence points to systematic sidelining of the importance of gender issues and an insufficient bloc of practitioners willing to own the subject. Moreover, an outdated, normative, and binary understanding of secularity's neutrality and religion's irrationality has rendered Western development organisations significantly religion-blind and skewed their sense of objectivity. A lack of knowledge, interest, and engagement with religion may have fostered an orientalist mindset that essentialises religion as backwards and subjective. Addressing personal attitudes and biases is crucial for enabling meaningful and more representative considerations of intersectional subjects. Much like gender, religion needs to be acknowledged as an intersectional subject, rather than being sidetracked and left to individual discretion.

Acknowledgement

This chapter is in part derived from an article published in *Development in Practice* on 30 May 2020. Copyright Taylor & Francis. Available online: www.tandfonline.com/doi/full/10.1080/09614524.2020.1760210

Bibliography

Abu-Lughod, L. (2002). Do Muslim Women Really Need Saving? Anthropological Reflections on Cultural Relativism and Its Others. *American Anthropologist*, 104(3): 783–790.

Casanova, J. (2009). Religion, Politics and Gender Equality: Public Religions Revisited. In Shahra Razavi (ed.), *A Debate on the Public Role of Religion and Its Social and Gender Implications*. Geneva: UN Research Institute for Social Development, Gender and Development Programme Paper.

Cornwall, A., Harrison, E., and Whitehead, A. (eds.). (2009). *Feminisms in Development: Contradictions, Contestations and Challenges*. London: Zed Books.

David, M. (2016). The Correspondence Theory of Truth. In Edward N. Zalta (ed.), *The Stanford Encyclopedia of Philosophy* (Fall 2016 Edition). Available from: https://plato.stanford.edu/archives/fall2016/entries/truth-correspondence/ [accessed 4 April 2019].

Deneulin, S., and Bano, M. (2009). *Religion in Development: Rewriting the Secular Script*. London: Zed Books.

Deneulin, S., and Rakodi, C. (2011). Revisiting Religion: Development Studies Thirty Years on. *World Development*, 39(1): 45–54.

Dinham, A. (2017). Religious Literacy in Public and Professional Settings. In Beth R. Crisp (ed.), *The Routledge Handbook of Religion, Spirituality and Social Work*. New York: Routledge.

Escobar, A. (2007). Worlds and Knowledges Otherwise. *Cultural Studies*, 21(2–3): 179–210.

Fiddian-Qasmiyeh, E. (2015). Engendering Understandings of Faith-Based Organisations: Intersections Between Religion and Gender in Development and Humanitarian Interventions. In Anne Coles, Leslie Gray, and Janet Momsen (eds.), *Routledge Handbook of Gender and Development*. London: Routledge.

Foucault, M. (1980). Truth and Power. In C. Gordon (ed.), *Power/Knowledge: Selected Interviews & Other Writings 1972–1977*. London: Harvester Press.

Jones, B., and Petersen, M. J. (2011). Instrumental, Narrow, Normative? Reviewing Recent Work on Religion and Development. *Third World Quarterly*, 32(7): 1291–1306.

Kimmel, M. (2002). *Toward a Pedagogy of the Oppressor*. Tikkun Magazine. Available from: www.fjaz.com/kimmel.html [accessed 13 February 2018].

Macleod, C. (2018). John Stuart Mill. In Edward N. Zalta (ed.). *The Stanford Encyclopedia of Philosophy*. Available from: https://plato.stanford.edu/archives/fall2018/entries/mill/ [accessed 14 July 2020].

Pelton, R. D. (1980). *The Trickster in West Africa: A Study of Mythic Irony and Sacred Delight*. Berkeley: University of California Press.

Prothero, S. (2007). *Religious Literacy: What Every American Needs to Know – And Doesn't*. San Francisco, CA: Harper San Francisco.

Radin, P. [1956] (1972). *The Trickster*. New York: Schocken Books.

Razavi, S. (1997). Fitting Gender into Development Institutions. *World Development*, 25(7): 1111–1125.

Ricketts, M. L. (1966). The North American Indian Trickster. *History of Religions*, 5: 327–350.

Rogers, E. M. (2003). *Diffusion of Innovations*. 5th Ed. New York: Free Press.

Said, E. (1978). *Orientalism*. New York: Pantheon Books.

Said, E. (2003). *Preface to the Twenty-Fifth-Anniversary Edition. Orientalism*. New York: Penguin.

Spivak, G. C. (1993). Can the Subaltern Speak? In Patrick Williams and Laura Chrisman (eds.), *Colonial Discourse and Postcolonial Theory*. New York: Harvester Wheatsheaf.

Tversky, A., and Kahneman, D. (1981). The Framing of Decisions and the Psychology of Choice. *Science*, 211(4481): 453–458.

Woodhead, L., and Catto, R. (eds.). (2012). *Religion and Change in Modern Britain*. London: Routledge.

World Bank Report. (2015). *Mind, Society, and Behavior*. Washington, DC: The World Bank Group.

7   Changing the sector

Enabling practitioners to drive internal change

Today, whether the intersection of religion and gender is addressed by development practitioners is largely left to their individual initiative. This chapter considers how practitioners can transform development organisations and catalyse the adoption of new ideas by their peers. The first part of the chapter reviews the conceptual roots of the term 'change agents' and examples from development practice. The second part of the chapter considers information homogeneity as a key barrier to innovation in development and proposes recruitment reforms as one mechanism to provide inclusive, practitioner-centred, and change-enabling environments.

The idea of change agents in current development practice

'Change agents' is not new as a concept in development. The term is frequently used in development reporting referring to individuals in beneficiary communities. Typically, development practice seeks to identify local change agents in beneficiary communities who have the networks and skills to encourage others to adopt desired changes. However, there is a noticeable void of development theory on the idea of change agents, and there is little mention in either practice or theory that considers change agents within development organisations themselves.

The concept of change agents originates from organisational studies and is considered essential to organisational change processes (see Beckhard, 1969; Bardach, 1977; Lunenburg, 2010; Andrews et al., 2010). The term was first used in Beckhard's (1969: 114) work *Organization development: strategies and models*. Today, Lunenburg's (2010: 5) definition is commonly used:

> [A]nyone who has the skill and power to stimulate, facilitate, and coordinate the change effort.

DOI: 10.4324/9781003112549-8

But the idea of change agents has been so liberally used that it lacks a coherent definition. It often appears in connection to or is used interchangeably with similar terms, such as change champions, change facilitator, drivers of change, or thought leaders.[1] There has been little systematic analysis of change management within development organisations, including the role of change agents and leadership theory more broadly. Andrews et al.'s (2010) brief examination of leadership-led change within development processes appears to be the exception. It is worth noticing the paradoxical nature of this research gap. There is a consensus within development theory that good programme leadership can significantly contribute to development outcomes and help transform the state institutions of developing countries. Development discourses centre on the idea of leading change. A look at development's vocabulary makes this visible. For example, frequently used expressions include 'drivers of change', 'community-led change', 'change agents', and 'theory of change'. All organisations interviewed for this book used the term 'change agent' in the context of local beneficiaries changing their communities' mindsets and behaviours. Change agents were crucial to lead – at times unpopular – development initiatives as well as convincing communities of health risks caused by harmful practices. Formally, women used to be popular change agents for gender equality. More recently, young men have been hailed as important change agents to challenge normalised gender norms and stereotypes. Today, FBOs and religious leaders are also considered to be vital change agents. One of my research participants explained 'that whole point of achieving personal transformation of religious leaders is key'. Notably, this personal transformation refers to change of beneficiaries, not development practitioners, and follows pre-defined development goals. Subsequently, most of the discourse on change in development is concerned with the change that development brings to other people, countries, and institutions, rather than the change it could and should drive within its own ranks. Holistic internal change within development organisations would include changes in recruitment, leadership strategies, team structures, conceptual understandings, research methods, resource allocation, and self-reflection. There are, in fact, many development practitioners who have attempted to generate such changes within their organisations. Yet, their struggles, opportunities, characteristics, and overall circumstances remain unexplored in both development theory and practice reports.

The occurrence of change within the scope of my research is difficult to prove. Nevertheless, according to the predominant conceptualisation of change agents, my research identified several participants that appear to act as internal change agents within their own organisations. Such change agents were noticeable across all three sample groups: women's rights activist, the staff of government aid agencies, and the staff of recipient organisations. They all seek to advance the understanding of the role of religion in gendered development approaches.

Example 1: Dina, women's rights activist, Lebanon and Syria

Dina's initial reaction to my research was similar to those of many of the women's rights activists in my sample: 'I am so glad you are doing this research'. She had noticed that there was a 'real need' to better understand this subject, especially after recently working with a European government-funded organisation on a project in several Middle Eastern countries. Dina told me that she always mentions the subject of religion whenever possible in her office because it is relevant in many of the situations they encounter as an organisation. As a minority woman of colour, she senses that it has been left up to her to bring these issues to the table. So far, she feels that her attempts to win colleagues' attention have not been successful. Dina grew up between Syria and Austria and has been exposed to different religions in different contexts with different gender expressions. She told me that she struggles daily with the overly simplistic depictions and ignorance when it comes to these complex issues.

Example 2: Jane, gender advisor, US recipient organisation

When I spoke with Jane, her organisation was scheduled to discuss the issue of religion and gender for the first time. She explained that this was enabled by her organisation's recent change in leadership:

So, your really timely question here is something that we hope to answer, as an aside, the president of [our organisation] comes from a religious organisation background. . . . When I raised the issue to him recently, that we'd like our next panel, Brown Bag, to be on faith-based organisations and gender-based violence, he was just hook, bait, and sinker. . . . He just wanted the whole heap.

Example 3: Aditi, local women's rights activist, India

At the time of my conversation with Aditi, her organisation had an internal staff policy to 'stay away from controversial issues'. She had struggled with this policy and recalled a few instances in which she nevertheless tried to challenge some of the religious misconceptions of the communities her organisation worked with:

I was having a chat with a Madrasa president and he said this: that women can't do theatre according to the Quran. And because I had worked with him for already eight months and I knew how he thinks, and he knew how I think, I was quickly able to tell him 'tell me where' because I have read the Quran through and through and I asked him 'tell me where, tell me where'.

Example 4: Gabriella, women's rights activist, Mexico

Gabriella's situation is fairly similar to Aditi's situation. Gabriella works with a local project in Mexico funded by a large international donor agency. In her free time, she is involved in a regional feminist activist network and recently attended a workshop series of the Latin American wing of Catholics for Choice. The workshops sought to provide arguments that reconcile 'sensitive' subjects like abortion, same-sex marriage, and incest with religion to foster meaningful conversations rather than mere alienation and discrimination. Gabriella emphasised that this workshop was not just for religious people or conveyed through a religious perspective. It focused on the recognition 'that religion is an important part of our context on how we can work forward with gender equality'. Gabriella spoke very passionately about both the workshops and the feminist network, which she said have helped her numerous times to cope with patriarchal religious leaders she encountered as part of her work.

Example 5: Gabriella's boss, recipient organisation, Mexico

Gabriella mentioned her boss to me several times. He is the national director of the development organisation she works with. He is a trained psychologist and was, therefore, 'really conscious about how religion had such a big impact on the beneficiaries, on the people that he was working with'. As a result, he adapted the interview questionnaire each beneficiary has to complete before joining the project. Because most beneficiaries were refugees with traumatic experiences, the admission interviews had a strong psychological component. Besides that, Gabriella's boss recently added a separate section on religion. Gabriella stressed several times that this was without the donor's knowledge or approval. It nevertheless seemed important to the director who argued that it is impossible to work 'with people of whom you do not understand or ignore this aspect of their lives'. At a different point in the interview, she also mentioned that her director was gay and his views on LGBTI issues conflicted strongly with the current wave of conservative politics and religious fundamentalism in Mexico. However, most of the time he found himself severely restricted to act on any of these issues, due to strict 'stay clear of controversy' donor policies.

Example 6: Nadine, gender advisor, government aid agency

This is an example mentioned earlier in the book. Nadine is the gender advisor of a European government who spent several decades in Indonesia and meanwhile arranged seminars on religion and gender on her own initiative. She is also involved with several local feminist activist groups in the country and also works for the local Ministry of Women's Empowerment and Child Protection.

In line with Lunenburg's (2010: 5) definition, most change agents identified in my research had the skill, and some the power, to achieve the change they wanted, even if only within their immediate environment. Examples 1 (Dina), 2 (Jane), 5 (Gabriella's Boss), and 6 (Nadine) seek to actively influence other members within the organisation to change their behaviour, while examples 3 (Aditi) and 4 (Gabriella) use their acquired knowledge to improve their own practice. This makes sense because Aditi and Gabriella find themselves at the end of a management line with arguably fewer connections and possibilities to influence others within their organisations. All of the examples had an additional feature in common which is absent in Luneburg's definition but appears critical: the will. As for the skill and power, these were often derived from change agents' access to non-redundant information. They bridge so-called 'structural holes' within their interpersonal networks. The structural holes argument is based on Burt's (1992) attempt to explain differences in social capital among members of a social network. The argument holds that change is more likely in social networks with gaps, as opposed to close-knit social groups or so-called 'network closure'. This is because close-knit social groups tend to have little access to diverse information and are generally bound together by upholding a strong traditional status quo. On the contrary, individuals who have access to outside social groups can access and learn new information and feed it back to their 'home' networks. These individuals have a comparative advantage when it comes to gaining knowledge. Therefore, they are arguably better positioned to become change agents. For instance:

Example 1: Dina is a local in the recipient country she works in but has also lived in the country of her European donor agency. She speaks both languages. She is personally convinced that the role of religion merits attention in staff briefings and project planning. Dina also has a rich network of human rights activists from her previous work assignments. Currently, she struggles to bring her unique knowledge into the organisation's work processes. She finds herself in a very tightly knit organisational structure, more like a system of network closure, and is almost always the only local, non-white, Muslim, and female person at the table.

Example 2: Jane's boss previously worked with gender as well as religious organisations. He is therefore interested in and knowledgeable about the intersection of the two subject areas. His support has enabled Jane to create space for knowledge sharing and influencing others within the organisation. Both, Jane and her boss could be considered change agents. In this case, it appears that Jane's boss bridges more structural holes and therefore can access more non-redundant information.

Example 3: Aditi works for a large development aid agency while also having strong links to members and leaders of relevant religious communities on both ends of the liberal-conservative spectrum. She understands their core religious pillars and has lived her entire life among them.

Example 4. Gabriella works for an international development organisation that does not consider the role of religion despite working in a country that she felt is experiencing a wave of religious fundamentalism. She also has close ties to a feminist activist network, which has granted her access to a more complex understanding of religion and its role in current social issues.

Example 5: Gabriella's boss is a psychologist who works closely with the beneficiaries of his organisation's projects and understands the role religion plays in their everyday lives. He also has ties to LGBTI movements and understands its goals and struggles.

Example 6: Nadine works in the Indonesian country office of a European government aid agency. She also works for the Indonesian Ministry of Women's Empowerment and Child Protection. She is half Indonesian, has lived many years in the country, and understands its language and culture. She frequently finds herself trying to bridge the aid agency's directives with the complex realities and needs on the grounds.

A network rich of structural holes can afford change agents access to nonredundant information, including opportunities for change that are not evident to others (Burt, 1992: 45). Additionally, structural holes present fewer normative constraints on how agents use information (Burt, 2004; Battilana and Casciaro, 2010). In other words, structural holes can provide freedom for practitioners to act on new information and implement change more easily. For example, Gabriella's boss was able to adapt a project questionnaire to better meet beneficiaries' needs. He was exposed to more knowledge and opportunities for change and had greater 'creative freedom from taken-for-granted institutional norms' to implement his visions (Battilana and Casciaro, 2010: 8). A development organisation as a whole may present a series of structural holes simply because of the nature of its globally distributed work processes and wide range of stakeholders. On the contrary, individual development organisations often display more homogenous systems of network closure, such as headquarter offices, country offices, or project sites. This may explain, why staff in headquarters have been slower to adopt GAD principles compared to some local activists on the ground.

Development's homogenous organisational structures: a 'disabling' environment?

As illustrated in this chapter, network closure (i.e., homogenous groups) allows little space for innovation. Over the past decades, the development industry has shown evidence of being an exclusive network. Large aid agencies, in particular, are known for their slow staff turnover and hierarchical staff structures. Once in the organisation, staff's skill sets are occasionally deemed so transferable that they may switch positions between two thematic areas with no substantial qualifications in either of them. Government aid departments in particular often use job rotation to reassign senior staff positions, leaving personnel with little gender expertise at the top of their departments. Such internal rotation together with the fact that many senior positions are held by the same people for decade-long periods limits outside information exposure and chances for structural change. When knowledge is produced by a relatively homogenous group of people, new ideas and behaviours struggle to find traction. Sherine, a research participant from Egypt told me about how excited she was to share ideas from her home country with her new colleagues at a UN agency headquarter last year. But she was met with more than mere resistance when she arrived. Her superior soon told her: 'you won't get your ideas done tomorrow when I had to wait decades to be heard. You've got to work for it'. She felt that even where the complex UN system would have allowed some degree of individual flexibility, some staff 'went out of their ways to make things complicated for others'. The working environment of many of the aid sectors' institutions has led practitioners to either be frustrated in their roles or leave the sector altogether. People of colour and minority backgrounds have reported especially exasperating experiences and difficulty breaking into development's exclusive ranks (Kagumire, 2020). Kagumire (2020) observed that both minority and local staff routinely experienced a combination of abuse of power and systemic sexism and racism. Kagumire writes that she herself felt like a diversity hire more than anything else:

> far from the rosy image of an industry 'doing good', I felt I was treated as a token black woman in a largely white male institution.

According to participants in my research, there is still a widespread assumption that locals are needed *in* the show but should not *run* the show. Local knowledge has often been described as 'local perspectives' or 'traditional knowledge', as opposed to Western knowledge which is considered to be 'scientific' and 'objective'. Contributions of locals have been systematically devalued through lower pay, fewer senior positions, and shorter contracts.

Changing recruitment requirements: a first step to transforming the sector

Since people are at the heart of both upholding and challenging systemic power imbalances, an important first step must be sweeping change within recruitment practices. Current recruitment practices are largely inadequate and open to bias and abuse (Anonymous, 2020). They have fostered a system in which people who are least affected by development issues are the ones making the decisions. My interview questions did not intend to explore recruitment specifically, but it nevertheless surfaced. One of my research participants, William, had worked extensively in project recruitment with a European recipient organisation. He was astonished and disillusioned on numerous occasions with the biases that influenced whether consultants were considered 'local' or 'internationals'. In practice, it was rare that someone from a developing country was considered an 'international consultant':

> It did not matter how much international exposure you had. If you were non-white and from the Global South, you could only ever be considered 'local' and would only be hired within your home country. If you were white, on the other hand, or from Europe or America, you were automatically considered an 'international', even if you had minimal or no significant experience outside your home country.

Whiteness then becomes interchangeable with credibility and some kind of cultural flexibility. Their knowledge and skill sets are considered neutral, easily transferable, and widely applicable. William noted that, on the contrary, non-white or local consultants are less likely to enjoy the same advantages. Their knowledge and skill sets are viewed as specialised to their current locality. They are rarely rotated to other areas:

> We would never send a gender expert from say Ghana to anywhere but Ghana. If you were from a so-called third world country, the boundaries of your career are the boundaries of your country. Your head only fits one hat. I am not saying there are no practitioners at all from developing countries who also get allocated to projects outside their countries. But it takes them a lot, a lot lot longer and twice the effort, I would say.

This was also found by a whistle-blower report in The Guardian's Global Development section:

> They ship around highly mobile young people, who have limited contextual or institutional knowledge' before hiring a local leader. [T]he prevalence and persistence of white international staff in senior leadership and the continued devaluing of local expertise and people, brings back echoes of the white civiliser, offering superior skills, convinced this is the natural and inevitable order of things.
>
> (Anonymous, 2020)

The same biases may exist for in-house recruitment. Maria, a project manager for a European recipient organisation, was a first-hand witness of this.

> I usually only do project recruitment, but it was an unusually busy time – just before Christmas – so I helped with some in-house recruitment. I spent a lot of time sourcing good candidates for multiple open roles in our project management unit. And then a few days later, I was informed that the senior manager of that division had actually already asked three of her friends from her previous work to join the team here. None of them had any significant international experience or something that qualified them distinctly for this job. I was super surprised and honestly quite a bit disappointed because I had found some good candidates. But everyone else seemed to accept this type of recruitment as normal.

Maria explained that recruitment bias became more visible to her after this incident: 'something as little as your accent when speaking English or your CV's formatting style could render you an outsider in development'. In contrast, 'white men in positions of power' rarely lost their jobs, even when reports accused them of discrimination or abuse of power. At the very most they were rotated to a different role (Kagumire, 2020).

A common way for development practitioners to dismiss discrimination claims is to argue that their 'entire work is underpinned by principles and values that promote equality and non-discrimination and that while we may not be perfect, we are far better than most' (Anonymous, 2020). But no one is immune to biases. There is a long-overdue need for the development sector to directly address these underlying power structures and take thoughtful steps to minimise their negative effects. Staffing politics can take priority over relevant factors, such as a candidates' knowledge about intersectional subjects like gender and religion. There is emphasis on gender in written documents, but to what extent are job candidates in practice actually required to prove a commitment to gender? As highlighted earlier in the book, mainstream staff do not typically have previous gender experience and even gender advisors often do not have academic gender backgrounds. There is a need for empirical research to assess the level to which staffing policies may influence the sidelining of certain subjects to mere checklists or external partnerships over conceptual and organisation-wide considerations.

Becoming a change agent is a political exercise that requires freedom, access, and power. Change is produced through continuous negotiation and persuasion and it strongly depends on ones' social standing and connections within a group. A good start for any practitioner would be to consider their own role and connection within their organisation, as well as any network gaps they are uniquely able to bridge outside their organisation. Guiding questions may be: 'what and who do I know that others do not?', 'what degree of freedom do I have within my workspace?', and 'what changes can I realistically affect?'. Many practitioners have little time, resources, or access to decision-makers. But practitioners can already affect great change by only adapting their own practice. For example, one can raise critical questions in meetings that challenge unconscious bias or review one's own research methods to grant the same nuance and complexity to gender realities abroad as at home. Practitioners can choose to be the one person in the group that does not let the team get away with century-old stereotypes, generalisations, or simplifications. They can also create a more enabling environment for change agents, for example, by acknowledging and supporting marginalised voices within their organisations. Those who have the opportunity to influence recruitment choices or partner selections can screen candidates for commitments to GAD principles.

Conclusion

The discussion of the religion–gender nexus is closely linked to the commitment of individual practitioners to it and the extent to which intra-organisational power dynamics dictate priorities, knowledge production, and recruitment processes. At present, development institutions continue to be more interested in changing *others* than *themselves*. Development prides itself on being a champion of enabling collective action and fighting inequality and discrimination worldwide. It can and should do the same for its own institutions. Practitioners have opportunities and responsibility for change. Development literature must also prioritise more research that theorises intra-organisational change and leadership within the development sector. This chapter highlights examples of change agents in the context of gender and religion. There is an opportunity for research to build on these examples and explore the role of change agents further, including best enabling environments. A research agenda concerned with the recruitment processes of development organisations appears vital in this regard. A recruitment reform could transform development in several ways: it could diversify the workforce and create a more inclusive sector, it could change how development knowledge is produced, it could challenge the current hierarchy between locals and internationals, and it could help speed up GAD mainstreaming by including gender in job specifications across the board.

Note

1 When discussing change agents, it is important to note that many organisational change theories speak of 'planned changes' (see Lippitt, 1958; Battilana and Casciaro, 2010) meaning they consider changes that are not controversial but overtly demanded and encouraged by organisations' leaderships.

Bibliography

Andrews, M., McConnell, J., and Wescott, A. (2010). *Development as Leadership-led Change*. HKS Faculty Research Working Paper Series, RWP10–009, John F. Kennedy School of Government, Harvard University.

Anonymous. (2020). The Aid Sector Must Do More to Tackle Its White Supremacy Problem. Global Development. *The Guardian*. Available from: www.theguardian.com/global-development/2020/jun/15/the-aid-sector-must-do-more-to-tackle-its-white-supremacy-problem [accessed 28 August 2020].

Bardach, E. (1977). *The Implementation Game*. Cambridge, MA: MIT Press.

Battilana, J., and Casciaro, T. (2010). *Power, Social Influence and Organizational Change: A Network Perspective*. Academy of Management Best Paper Proceedings.

Beckhard, R. (1969). *Organization Development: Strategies and Models*. Reading, MA: Addison-Wesley.

Burt, R. S. (1992). *Structural Holes: The Social Structure of Competition*. Cambridge, MA: Harvard University Press.

Burt, R. S. (2004). Structural Holes and Good Ideas. *American Journal of Sociology*, 110(2): 349–399.

Kagumire, R. (2020). It's Time the UN Faced Up to Its Treatment of Black People Like Me. Global Development. *The Guardian*. Available from: www.theguardian. com/global-development/2020/jul/06/its-time-the-un-faced-up-to-its-treatment-of-black-people-like-me [accessed 28 August 2020].

Lippitt, R. (1958). *The Dynamics of Planned Change*. New York: Harcourt, Brace.

Lunenburg, F. C. (2010). Managing Change: The Role of the Change Agent. *International Journal of Management, Business, and Administration*, 13(1).

Concluding remarks

The research findings presented in this book suggest that a religiously literate understanding of the religion–gender nexus is indispensable for development policymakers and practitioners. Development organisations struggle to navigate complex societal norms, conflicting belief systems, political agendas, and conservative backlash. As such, the following three areas merit immediate attention:

Encouraging self-reflective religious literacy: Given the global relevance of the religion–gender nexus, it is no longer enough to engage with religions only via external partnerships. Development organisations should ensure that all staff are trained in basic religious literacy including:

- Understanding that religious discourses, like all discourses, are not static, but context specific, historically situated, internally contested, and continually reinforced and altered. The same religion is being practised differently in different places.
- Acknowledging that in many cases it is difficult to define the extent to which practices have religious origins. Practices that are described as religious by some people may be considered cultural, traditional, or simply patriarchal by other people of the same religious group. Generalisations and simplifications in the context of religion produce single – often conservative – religious narratives and may overshadow more moderate or progressive standpoints within the same religion.
- Recognising how religions interact with gender norms and how religions are appropriated to legitimise norms as God-ordained, making them seem unchangeable. Gender norms in religious settings are just as constructed, normalised, internalised, and reproduced as in any other contexts.
- Understanding how patriarchal and religious power structures are interlinked. There is a reason why some religious interpretations are more dominant than others in a given location. The way religion is interpreted

DOI: 10.4324/9781003112549-9

mirrors existing power structures. Women may also enact and benefit from patriarchal norms or support conservative or fundamentalist interpretations of religion. Therefore, increasing female participation alone or partnering with female actors will not automatically generate more 'women-friendly' results.

• Acknowledging the fluidity of religious knowledge production and supporting the democratisation of such processes by supporting marginalised feminist voices and interpretations.
• Understanding religious legislations across different contexts and how it is produced. For example, overlooking or perpetuating the deliberate confusion of Islamic law and *Shariah* almost always has disastrous effects for women.
• Recognising the limitations of religious literacy and the importance of self-reflection. Any lens of studying religion can only offer a partial and context-specific viewpoint. For example, studying lived Islam in a village of the Batna Province of Algeria will unlikely provide knowledge on lived Islam in parts of Indonesia or Turkey. Furthermore, no one automatically possesses religious literacy. Religious literacy is not the same as 'being religious'. Likewise, not 'being religious' does not provide a more neutral starting point for becoming religiously literate. Religious literacy is as much about knowledge as it is about critical self-awareness and acknowledging that perspectives about religions vary widely. Finally, since religions are complex, boundless, and ever changing, religious literacy ought to be a context-specific and continuous learning process, too.

Forming gender-focused partnerships: Understanding the complex ways in which gender and religion interact and shape gendered power dynamics in specific contexts can inform better partner selection. Development has a long history of partnering with international and grassroots organisations. Partnering with any organisation – religious or non-religious – supports the organisation's legitimacy, its access to resources, and its ideology, including on gender issues. As part of the collective effort it will take to realise the SDG 5, all partners – whether religious or not – should be selected based on their track record on gender equality issues. Gender and development scholars recommend that, ideally, partners are at the forefront of achieving gender equality within their own contexts. Subsequently, there are two challenges development organisations must prepare for:

1   Sometimes gender-progressive or feminist organisations are hesitant to engage with foreign secular organisations in fear of being branded 'Western agents' which would delegitimise them in the eyes of the

very local religious authority they seek to challenge. Regardless of this, development organisations would be well advised to continuously identify feminist and women's rights organisations and attempt partnerships with them. At the very least, development practitioners can learn from these organisations to build their own religious literacy and understanding of how religion interacts with gender in specific contexts. However, government aid agencies who themselves are permeated by conservative gender discourses may struggle to convincingly advocate for gender equality and transformative change abroad.

2   Western development agencies have a track record of forming strategic or politically palatable partnerships. In practice, this has meant prioritising partnerships with dominant – often male – actors who are gatekeepers to large sections of the local community. A desire for short-term efficacy has in some cases led to negative effects in the long term, especially because the religious actors with the biggest networks and influence do not necessarily hold the most gender-progressive opinions. This presents an inconvenient trade-off for traditional development approaches, which now – more than ever – need to prove their commitment to gender equality. An additional challenge will be to partner with marginalised feminist voices and to speak out against gender injustice – including misogynistic distortions of religion – more boldly without alienating conservative fractions of the community.

Conducting comprehensive gender analyses *prior* to project implementation and partner selection: Despite global policy mandates to conduct gender analyses and the abundance of theoretical tools to do so, gender analyses of major development organisations are still insufficient and ill-equipped to identify and comprehend the complex expressions of gender and religion. Gender practitioners struggle to gain support and attention from mainstream staff and organisations' leaderships and are not involved in the selection of development partners. Gender studies are often little understood by project leaders and sometimes they are not read at all. A comprehensive and conceptually based gender analysis can illustrate the religion–gender intersections in a given context. Such analysis can reveal structural inequalities and power dynamics that permeate both high- and low-income countries. It can enable better programme design and facilitate the inclusion of religious actors. It can also draw attention to the intersectionality of gender inequality. A consideration of intersectionality provides a more nuanced and truthful picture of complex gender inequalities. However, it requires skilled gender advisors and committed project leaders and staff across all levels of development.

Transforming attitudes and creating an equal playing field within the development sector: My research indicates that Western development continues to hide under the cloak of secularism without a self-reflective and critical analysis of its own religious ties and influences. Convinced of its own neutrality, the sector has been slow in addressing practitioners' and institutional biases.

Contrary to global policy pushes, practitioners show an overwhelming reluctance to engage with religion in practice and it continues to be largely left to individual discretion. Any effort to build religious literacy within development organisations must begin with overcoming the reluctance towards intersectional subjects. In addition, knowledge production has to be diversified and decolonised. Local and minority voices continue to be undervalued through lower positions and pay. In its 75th year, the development sector must address the unequal and toxic power balance at its heart. In addition to critical self-reflection, structural change is needed including bias awareness training, a revised recruitment processes, and openness to outside scrutiny.

This book has argued that issues related to religion and gender are complex and span the entire globe. Gender norms in the Global South cannot be expected to have fewer root causes than gender norms in the Global North or be expected to change within the space of just one development intervention. Identifying – often unconscious – gender norms is an incredibly difficult and time-consuming process. Even unlearning one's own internalised gendered behaviour may take a lifetime. Transforming gender power structures of an entire society is known to take generations. Moreover, a rising tide of political religion that is fixated on gender issues has further complicated the boundaries between patriarchy and religion. Quick fixes in development stand in paradoxical contrast to the fact that Western countries have also taken centuries to shift gender norms with almost all of them still at the task. But this does not mean that development practitioners cannot make meaningful contributions. With a conceptual understanding of gendered power dynamics, self-reflective religious literacy, and a healthy level of humility, there are opportunities for change. For example, an improved partner selection can identify and support local actors that are already fighting for transformative gender change. At the very least, a rigorous and truthful gender analysis can allow practitioners to avoid doing further harm by misrepresenting complex dynamics or emboldening conservative voices.

Appendix

1 Interview participants

Name[1]	Role[2]	Organisation	Region[3]
Samantha	Gender Advisor	Government Aid Agency	North America
Lisa	Gender Advisor	Government Aid Agency	Europe
Elizabeth	Gender Advisor	Government Aid Agency	Europe
Christian	Gender Advisor	Government Aid Agency	Europe
Ellen	Gender Advisor	Government Aid Agency	Europe
Simone	Religion Advisor	Government Aid Agency	Europe
Patrick	Lead on Faith and Civil Society	Government Aid Agency	Europe
Nadine	Gender Advisor	Government Aid Agency and Women's Rights Activist	Europe and Indonesia
Jennifer	Gender Advisor	Recipient Organisation	Germany
William	Business Development Manager	Recipient Organisation	UK
Claire	Gender Director	Recipient Organisation	UK
Maria	Project Manager (Gender)	Recipient Organisation	UK
Marlene	Advisor on Women's Rights and Religious Fundamentalism	Recipient Organisation and Women's Rights Activist	UK and Canada
Cheryl	Director of Gender	Recipient Organisation	USA
Amelia	Gender Advisor	Recipient Organisation	USA
Jane	Faith Advisor	Recipient Organisation	USA
Sherine	Women's Rights Activist	Independent	Egypt
Gina	Women's Rights Activist	Independent	Egypt and Guatemala
Dina	Women's Rights Activist	Independent and Recipient Organisation	Lebanon and Syria

Name[1]	Role[2]	Organisation	Region[3]
Aditi	Women's Rights Activist	Independent and Recipient Organisation	India
Nandi	Women's Rights Activist	Independent	India
Nabila	Women's Rights Activist	Independent	Malawi
Gabriella	Women's Rights Activist	Independent	Mexico
Salma	Women's Rights Activist	Independent	Morocco and Malaysia

2 Document categories for analysis

Document Type[4]	Organisation	Quantity
Gender Strategy	Government Aid Agencies	9
Gender Tools/Frameworks	Government Aid Agencies	3
Country Strategy (incl. Mexico, Egypt, Morocco, Malawi, Zambia, Ethiopia, Kenya, the Philippines, Malaysia, and India)	Government Aid Agencies	16
Policy Briefs (on gender, social norms, or religion)	Government Aid Agencies	14
Terms of Reference (for specific gender projects)	Government Aid Agencies	9
Evaluations of Gender Programming	Government Aid Agencies	5
Strategy Document/Statement on Religious Partners	Government Aid Agencies	6
Gender Policy	Recipient Organisations	5
Gender Analysis	Recipient Organisations	6
Thematic Reports on Gender and Social Norms	Recipient Organisations	5
Thematic Reports on Religion and Gender	Recipient Organisations	21
Gender Strategies and Guidelines	Faith-Based Organisations	5
Total		**102**

Notes

1 All names have been changed for confidentiality purposes.
2 All gender participants were either directors of their departments or senior advisors.
3 To maintain anonymity of government aid agencies, their home regions rather than countries are indicated.
4 The most recent available versions were used.

Index

Note: Page numbers in *italics* indicate a figure on the corresponding page.

For Product Safety Concerns and Information please contact our EU
representative GPSR@taylorandfrancis.com
Taylor & Francis Verlag GmbH, Kaufingerstraße 24, 80331 München, Germany